KU-759-192

THE DOCTORS

The first *Doctor Who Annual* was published in 1965, introducing readers to what it called the "citizen of all Space and Time" in a two-page feature called Who is Dr Who?

"No one knows where he came from," said the article. "He is human in shape and speech and manner. He appears to be old and feeble and at the same time young and strong and active, as though the normal processes of ageing had passed him by."

Two years later there was a new Doctor, and the latest annual sought to explain the transformation in a piece entitled Phoenix in the TARDIS. "In his previous personality he enjoyed nine hundred years of stupendous adventures in his marvellous vessel the Time and Relative Dimensions in Space craft. The mind might reel at what lies ahead for the regenerated Doctor."

In subsequent decades *Doctor Who* became such an institution that we spent rather less time analysing its lead character. For the third volume of our 50th anniversary publications we have resurrected that questioning spirit for a journey through the lives of all 11 Doctors, and the actors who played them.

Mark Gatiss describes his fascination with the First Doctor and former script editor Andrew Cartmel compares his own approach to the series with that of his predecessors and current showrunner Steven Moffat. Elsewhere, we visit a parallel universe where anniversaries past were commemorated not by *The Three Doctors*, *The Five Doctors* and *Dimensions in Time*, but with the unmade stories *Deathworld*, *The Six Doctors* and *The Dark Dimension*.

Our celebration of the latest anniversary comes to a close with an introduction to Peter Capaldi – the actor who will take this remarkable saga into the future.

Happy birthday *Doctor Who*!

Marcus

EDITOR
MARCUS HEARN

ART EDITOR
PERI GODBOLD

EDITORS FOR DWM
TOM SPILSBURY, PETER WARE

PICTURE RESEARCH
DEREK HANDLEY

SPECIAL THANKS
JONATHAN RIGBY

Managing Director	MIKE RIDDELL
Managing Editor	ALAN O'KEEFE
Head of Production	MARK IRVINE
Production Assistant	JEZ METEYARD
Circulation and Trade	
Marketing Controller	KATE WILKINSON
Head of Marketing	JESS TADMOR
Marketing Executive	JESS DORAN

THANKS TO:
BBC Wales, the BBC Written Archive Centre, bbc.co.uk, Andrew Beech, Kit Bevan, Richard Bignell; Piers Britton; Dominitemporal Services, Martin Gainsford, Andrew Ledger, Grace Lessner (New Hampshire Public Television), Jeff Lyons, Steven Moffat, Tim Morgan, David Richardson, Carole Robertson, Nigel Robinson, Paul Taylor and Jo Ware.

ADVERTISING
Madison Bell
Telephone 0207 389 0835
Email damien.tidd@madisonbell.com

madison bell INDEPENDENT MEDIA SELLING

Doctor Who 50 Years™ Issue #3 The Doctors Published October 2013 by Panini UK Ltd, under licence from BBC Worldwide. Office of publication: Panini UK Ltd, Brockbourne House, 77 Mount Ephraim, Tunbridge Wells, Kent, TN4 8BS. All *Doctor Who* material is © BBCtv 2013. *Doctor Who* logo ™ & © BBC 2012. Daleks © Terry Nation. All other material is © Panini UK Ltd unless otherwise indicated. No similarity between any of the fictional names, characters persons and/or institutions herein with those of any living or dead persons or institutions is intended and any such similarity is purely coincidental. Nothing may be reproduced by any means in whole or part without the written permission of the publishers. This periodical may not be sold, except by authorised dealers, and is sold subject to the condition that it shall not be sold or distributed with any part of its cover or markings removed, nor in a mutilated condition. The publishers cannot be held responsible for unsolicited manuscripts, photographs or artwork. Newstrade distribution: Marketforce (UK) Ltd 020 3148 3333. ISSN 2052-3840.

PANINI MAGAZINES

BBC

MIX
Paper
FSC FSC® C010219

CONTENTS

A page from a BBC Enterprises sales brochure published in 1965.

WILLIAM HARTNELL

The role of the original Doctor would transform perceptions of actor William Hartnell. It was the final milestone in a distinguished career.

FEATURE BY **JONATHAN RIGBY**

Tucked away inside the 16 June 1964 edition of *Radio Times* was an engaging little piece called *The Man Who's Who*. In it, the anonymous author speculated on the identity of the actor playing the lead role in the wildly popular BBC series *Doctor Who*.

It was no secret, of course, that his name was William Hartnell – but his latest role was quite unlike anything he had done before. After all, prior to *Doctor Who*, audiences had known him as a very different type of character, to such a degree he felt typecast.

Ever since playing the hard-as-nails Sgt Ned Fletcher in Carol Reed's classic 1944 film *The Way Ahead*, Hartnell's supposed 'identity' had been set in stone, certainly as far as casting directors were concerned. He was the grim-faced, inflexible tough guy, barking out orders and withering subordinates with a single look. "Long after the guns had fallen silent," noted the *Radio Times* writer, "he was still soldiering on... with stripes neatly blancoed, beret at regulation angle and tight mouth emitting regulation noises."

Doctor Who, however, had changed all that, giving Hartnell the new identity he craved. "I've waited for years to do something like this," he claimed, "and I have never been happier."

If *Doctor Who* came as a boon to Hartnell, there's no doubt that Hartnell was himself a boon to *Doctor Who*. Here was one of British cinema's greatest character actors, his thin-lipped countenance known to millions, lending gravitas – and the cinema-honed skills of a master technician – to what started out as a mere Saturday teatime diversion for children.

"I knew – I just knew – that *Doctor Who* was going to be an enormous success," he pointed out in 1973. "I believed in it. I remember telling producer Verity Lambert right at the start, 'This is going to run for five years.' And now it's ten years old."

Now, of course, it's 50 years old – a five-decade run that would be inconceivable without the pioneering achievements of William Hartnell between 1963 and 1966.

Though the application of a lengthy white wig suggested someone closer to 70, Hartnell was actually 55 when he took on *Doctor Who*. He was an only child, born in the St Pancras area of north London on 8 January 1908; he was also illegitimate. Having found a surrogate father in the philanthropic artist Hugh Blaker, he signed up, aged 17, with the touring troupe operated by ageing actor-manager Sir Frank Benson.

Styling himself Billy rather than William at this early stage, Hartnell made a name for himself in the 1930s principally as a stage farceur, but also in the kind of fleabitten British films ▶

"I REMEMBER TELLING PRODUCER VERITY LAMBERT RIGHT AT THE START, 'THIS IS GOING TO RUN FOR FIVE YEARS.'"

HARTNELL PERFECTED A MERCURIAL MIX OF WASPISHNESS, SAGACITY AND PAWKY HUMOUR.

Top: As Inspector Roberts, alongside Ray Barrett in the 1963 film *To Have and to Hold*. Hartnell and Barrett would be reunited in the 1965 *Doctor Who* story *The Rescue*.

Top right: William Russell (as Ian Chesterton) and Hartnell pictured during the making of *Five Hundred Eyes*, the third episode of *Marco Polo* (1964).

Above: The Doctor, Susan (Carole Ann Ford) and Ian are cornered by strange armoured creatures in *The Survivors*, the second episode of *The Mutants* (aka *The Daleks*, 1963-64).

Right: A signed postcard featuring a portrait from *The Firemaker*, the final episode of *100,000 BC* (aka *An Unearthly Child*, 1963).

◄ then known as quota quickies. By the end of the decade he'd become a fixture at Teddington Studios, where a better class of quota quickie was being made by the British arm of Warner Bros. According to Hartnell's widow Heather, plans were afoot to transport Billy to Hollywood. But then the war intervened.

After a spell in the Tank Corps, Hartnell was cast opposite the young Richard Attenborough in *Brighton Rock*, which played at London's Garrick Theatre in 1943. Carol Reed saw the show and immediately cast Hartnell in *The Way Ahead*. Top billing followed in a number of minor post-war films, and by March 1947 Hartnell was at Welwyn Studios for the Boulting Brothers' screen version of *Brighton Rock*, in which he once again played the sinister seaside gangster Dallow.

In June 1950, Hartnell appeared at the Apollo Theatre in the Hugh Hastings comedy *Seagulls Over Sorrento*. Though the play was to run for four years, there were signs straight away that Hartnell wasn't entirely comfortable with the disciplinarian blowhards he was being called upon to portray. "Mr William Hartnell cannot quite make us believe in the unrelenting tyranny of the petty officer," commented Peter Fleming in *The Spectator*, "but he acts the part for all it is worth."

It was in June 1957 that Hartnell first appeared in the Granada sitcom *The Army Game*, making such a hit as Sgt-Major Bullimore [sic] that by March the following year he was cast in an almost identical role in the first Carry On comedy, *Carry On Sergeant*, receiving top billing for his pains. But it was only with the 1963 film *This Sporting Life* – in which Lindsay Anderson

cast him, in Hartnell's words, as "rather an ill and useless old man" – that he was able to break out of the 'heavy' mode.

It was while watching Anderson's film that Verity Lambert suddenly realised who she wanted for *Doctor Who*. Hartnell agreed to play the role that July, and by December, after only two episodes had been screened, *The Stage* was enthusiastically describing his Doctor as "a pastiche of absent-minded professor, space age scientist and medieval wizard." Hartnell's own formulation was more straightforward: "I represent a cross between the Wizard of Oz and Father Christmas."

Trimly frock-coated and occasionally fitted with an astrakhan hat, Hartnell perfected a mercurial mix of waspishness, sagacity and pawky humour, together with a substantial side-order of capriciousness and calculated irresponsibility. With the Doctor's origin as a Time Lord as yet undreamed of, he was able to retain a genuine sense of mystique – just 'who' was this mysterious time traveller? And he could bring a bewitching sense of otherness to the rare moments when a back-story was hinted at, as in *The Massacre of St Bartholomew's Eve* in February 1966: "Perhaps I should go home. Back to my own planet. But I can't..."

Hartnell delighted, in particular, in the opportunity to entertain children, whom he adored; in his numerous (unpaid) public appearances he became a kind of Pied Piper figure to the swarms of young fans who turned up. The series' gruelling 48-weeks-a-year schedule was another matter, however, and on top of this he was succumbing to (yet to be diagnosed) arteriosclerosis.

The vascular dementia arising from this resulted in occasionally garbled line readings that the BBC broadcast regardless, blunting the impact of a performance that had once been so electrifying. The condition also brought with it an emotional volatility that made Hartnell's later stories a trial for any co-workers who rubbed him up the wrong way. "My role was to laugh Bill out of his five or six tempers a day," recalled Maureen O'Brien, who played Vicki. "He was a charming creature in spite of his irascibility, and those terrible teeth that he used to bare when he was angry."

"I think I'll be doing it for many years," Hartnell predicted on *Desert Island Discs* in August 1965. By the following year, however, the decision had been made to continue *Doctor Who* without him. Hartnell agreed to go on 16 July; he recorded his final appearance, in the concluding episode of *The Tenth Planet*, on 8 October.

"I think three years in one part is a good innings," he told *The Times*, "and it is time for a change." In reality he was distraught. "I didn't willingly give up the part," he told an admirer in 1968. "BBC planners forced me to retire."

In later years Hartnell took a few TV and theatre parts but became increasingly enfeebled. As a result his role opposite Jon Pertwee and Patrick Troughton in *The Three Doctors*, shot in November 1972, had to be considerably reduced. Not long afterwards, on 23 April 1975, he died of heart failure, aged 67.

His legacy is obvious, and vast. The Doctor was his dream role and his inspired characterisation enchanted many millions around the world. Thanks to him, one of the First Doctor's final pronouncements now has a prophetic ring.

"It isn't all over," he tells Michael Craze's disbelieving Ben in *The Tenth Planet*. "It's far from being all over…" ✳

Top: *The Massacre of St Bartholomew's Eve* (1966) required Hartnell to play both the Doctor (pictured) and the villainous Abbot of Amboise.

Above: One of several caricatures of Hartnell as the Doctor that featured in the *BBC Book of Crackerjack*, published in 1966.

Right: Propping up the bar with Richard Harris in *This Sporting Life* (1963).

THE WAY AHEAD (1944)
Hartnell's tough performance in this documentary-style hit made him a name to conjure with, leading to star billing in such pictures as *The Agitator*, *Strawberry Roan*, *Murder in Reverse?* and *Appointment with Crime*.

BRIGHTON ROCK (1947)
Hartnell's dead-eyed Dallow and Richard Attenborough's razor-slashed Pinkie remain arguably the most iconic faces of British film noir. Hartnell's fan club was inaugurated towards the end of filming, in summer 1947.

THE RINGER (1952)
Guy Hamilton's version of the much-filmed Edgar Wallace thriller saw Hartnell inheriting the role of whimsical petty crook Sam Hackett from Cockney favourites Gordon Harker and Ronald Shiner.

THE ARMY GAME
(1957-58, 1960-61)
Hartnell's CSM Percy Bullimore, terrorising the hapless conscripts of Hut 29 at Nether Hopping, appeared in three series of this hit Granada comedy, inspired by the 1956 film *Private's Progress* (in which Hartnell also appeared).

CARRY ON SERGEANT
(1958)
Hartnell didn't just play a vital role in launching *Doctor Who*; he also helped launch the evergreen Carry On comedies. In this first one – clearly inspired by *The Army Game* – he was the star attraction as the titular Sgt Grimshaw.

THIS SPORTING LIFE (1963)
The role of dissipated hanger-on to Richard Harris' rugby forward in this New Wave drama – together with Sylvia Syms' father in *The World Ten Times Over*, released later the same year – helped break Hartnell's typecasting.

SCRIPTING THE FIRST DOCTOR

The original TARDIS crew were cautious travellers whose adventures often separated them from the safety of their ship.

FEATURE BY **JUSTIN RICHARDS**

Of course, there is no such thing as a 'typical' *Doctor Who* story – that's what makes the programme so exciting and fresh. But there are narrative elements over and above the character of the Doctor himself that define each Doctor's time in the role.

So, if we were to attempt the impossible and craft the archetypal First Doctor story, what might it involve?

The fundamental characteristic of most First Doctor stories is that the Doctor and his companions are unwilling adventurers. Not only is the TARDIS' destination unpredictable and apparently random, but once he's arrived the Doctor is generally reluctant to get involved. If he had his way, nine times out of ten he'd get back inside the TARDIS as soon as his initial curiosity is satisfied. So something has to happen to prevent this.

Most often, the TARDIS simply becomes inaccessible. The bulk of the very first story, *100,000 BC* (1963), simply chronicles the

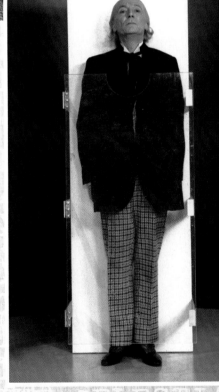

BECAUSE OF HIS RELATIVE FRAILTY, HARTNELL'S DOCTOR IS RARELY AT THE CENTRE OF THE ACTION.

Doctor's attempts to escape the Tribe of Gum and return to the TARDIS. *Marco Polo* (1964) sees the TARDIS key surrendered. Often, as in *The Dalek Invasion of Earth* (1964), there is a physical impediment to returning to the ship. Other times, as in that very first story, one or more of the travellers is captured.

On the one occasion when the Doctor manufactures an excuse not to leave, in the first Dalek story *The Mutants* (1963-64), he soon realises this was a bad move. There's no doubt that if he still had the vital TARDIS fluid link the Doctor would leave Skaro, abandoning the Thals to their fate.

One of the more imaginative reasons for the Doctor and his friends to be caught up in events is the TARDIS jumping a time track, as happens in *The Space Museum* (1965). The Doctor must stay in order to ensure that the future he and his friends have glimpsed – of themselves as museum exhibits – never comes to pass.

A consequence of this general unwillingness to get involved is that the Doctor himself is rarely the centre of the story. Again, there are exceptions like *The Chase* (1965), where the Daleks pursue the TARDIS through space and time. But generally the Doctor is caught up in events and situations that are already taking place.

Once the initial quest to get Ian and Barbara home is completed, the Doctor does tend to get involved more willingly. By the end of his era, he will even act on a hunch and seek out possible trouble in *The War Machines* (1966), but this is very much the exception rather than the rule. In his final story, *The Tenth Planet* (1966), he remains content for the most part to be an observer, allowing events to unfold as he knows they must.

Indeed, because of his age and relative frailty, William Hartnell's Doctor is rarely at the centre of the action – any fights and physical business being handled by his younger companions (usually Ian, Steven or later Ben as the 'young male lead'). As well as this being a physical necessity, it also fits with the Doctor's underlying philosophy of not harming others unless he is himself threatened. Although, as ever, there are exceptions even to this.

So, back to that archetypal First Doctor story. It might start with the Doctor and his friends being denied access to the TARDIS, then getting caught up in local events, typically a struggle between two opposing factions – Zarbi and Menoptra, Daleks and Thals, Greeks and Trojans, Rills and Drahvins... As events progress, seemingly out of the Doctor's control, he slowly emerges as the voice of reason, advocating the

path of least resistance in affecting a settlement between the factions. A settlement that often means the oppressor is finally dealt with and justice prevails.

The exceptions to such a neat ending tend to be where history teaches us differently, be it the regime of *The Aztecs* (1964), the Trojan War of *The Myth Makers* (1965), or the horrendous *Massacre of St Bartholomew's Eve* (1966). The First Doctor is generally reluctant to rewrite established history – as he tells Barbara, "not one line." ✳

FIRST LOVE

In the new BBC drama *An Adventure in Space and Time*, writer Mark Gatiss set out to tell the poignant story of First Doctor William Hartnell.

INTERVIEW BY **MARCUS HEARN**

Much of the anticipation surrounding *An Adventure in Space and Time* focused on its evocation of the seminal period in 1963 that led to the creation of *Doctor Who*. While it's true that the film includes such legendary figures as producer Verity Lambert (played by Jessica Raine), original director Waris Hussein (Sacha Dhawan) and co-creator Sydney Newman (Brian Cox), writer Mark Gatiss points out that his long-cherished production is as much the story of the First Doctor, William Hartnell, played by David Bradley.

The idea of dramatising the events surrounding the birth of the series first occurred to Gatiss in the mid-1990s. He was partly inspired by *The Fools on the Hill*, a 1986 BBC production that recreated the opening night of British television 50 years earlier. Gatiss returned to his *Doctor Who* idea prior to the show's 40th anniversary, but the timing was once again not right.

"I had a brief discussion with the executives at Television Centre," he recalls, "and realised that it was only going to be conceivable on the level of a DVD extra," he says. "A bit like *The Mind Robber*, everything would have taken place in a white-walled studio, with imagined scenes from William Hartnell's life."

The idea resurfaced in 2009, by which time *Doctor Who* was more highly regarded by the BBC. Four years later it finally became a reality, but only after Gatiss revised his screenplay. "I felt that there were numerous threads, each of which could justify a drama in itself, but over the course of eight, nine or ten drafts I focused it to work out which of those stories it had to be. Fundamentally, it had to be Bill Hartnell's story.

"As soon as I knew that he couldn't remember his lines and that he was eventually eased out, the story's *Death of a Salesman* quality began to appeal to me. Here was a man who wasn't sure if he should even take on the role of the Doctor, made a huge success of it against the odds, and then had it taken away from him. A bit like getting what you've always wanted for Christmas and then having to give it straight back.

"But I didn't want this to be the miseryfest that biopics sometimes are, so I focused on the fact that Hartnell's greatest gift to the show was that he left it early. This introduced the concept of having other Doctors. Hartnell predicted the show would last for five years, and if he'd been well it probably would've done. But it might not have carried on with other Doctors. It would've stopped, and would now be one of those old shows that's only vaguely remembered."

Hartnell's tenure came to an end in 1966 for reasons that weren't even hinted at for several years. His irascible and unpredictable behaviour – aggravated by the onset of serious illness – made him unpopular with some of his co-stars and members of the production team.

"We don't pull our punches about the fact that Bill could be frustrating and difficult, and couldn't always remember his lines. I reined in some of the other things about his personality that we all know about." This, of course, is a veiled reference to some of the actor's widely reported prejudices.

"An awful lot of people of his generation, and of his working class background, would've held similar views," says Gatiss, quick to contextualise Hartnell's behaviour. "I think if my grandfather had played Doctor Who he would've been the same. I knew that Hartnell liked Waris Hussein, so I asked him, 'Do you think you were the *right kind* of Indian?' And he told me he thought that was absolutely it. Bill was the type of man who would mutter over his *Daily Mail* about immigrants, ▶

TURNING BACK TIME

Gatiss admits it was difficult deciding which episodes to recreate in *An Adventure in Space and Time*. "I thought we had to do a bit of *The Web Planet*," he says, "because it was so fantastically ambitious and illustrated where the show was going. I wanted a good bit of history, to show that was part of the original format, so we have bits of *Marco Polo* and *The Reign of Terror* in there as well.

"One scene I had in my mind from the beginning was to recreate Bill's speech from the end of *The Massacre of St Bartholomew's Eve* – 'Now they've all gone... None of them could understand...' – because it occurred to me that it worked on two levels. It's a clip from a great episode, but it's also about him and his isolation. That's one of my favourite scenes.

"I had such ambitions, but I'm afraid budgetary restrictions knocked most of them on the head. One that didn't come off

was a sequence from the end of *The Daleks' Master Plan*. I wanted a Sara Kingdom double running away from the ageing effects of the Time Destructor, and when she turns around... it's Jean Marsh! Jean actually agreed to do it, but we had to cut it because we couldn't afford it."

Above: Mark Gatiss in a publicity shot from his 2012 documentary *Horror Europa*. Photo by Matthew Thomas.

Left: The Doctor (William Hartnell) and Ian Chesterton explore Vortis in the first episode of *The Web Planet* (1965).

Below left: Sara Kingdom meets a grisly end in *Destruction of Time*, the final episode of *The Daleks' Master Plan* (1965-66).

but then when he met someone he admired he would make an exception and say, 'Oh, but *he's* all right.' That to me is a rather familiar British racism.

"I think there's been a great focus on these aspects of Bill's character simply because he played the Doctor," Gatiss adds. "It's just that we don't like the fact that the person who played Doctor Who didn't have the same politics as the Doctor."

Given that *An Adventure in Space and Time* will probably become the most significant memento of Hartnell's life and career, does Gatiss feel a sense of responsibility towards his subject – a man he never actually met?

"Very much," he says emphatically. "I think it's a very moving story, and I became very fond of him. In the first couple of drafts there was a lot more about his childhood, because I was fascinated by it and his obsession with his illegitimacy. There was a bit more about his affairs as well, but eventually I focused it down to just a couple of little references because otherwise it risked becoming extremely miserable and looking like a hatchet job. The film was produced as part of the anniversary, and I wanted it to be celebratory."

Gatiss nevertheless arrived at the belief that Hartnell was definitely ousted from the role of the Doctor.

"I did a long interview with [former *Doctor Who* story editor] Donald Tosh," he says, "where he talked about how

> ## "FOR BILL HARTNELL, TO HAVE BECOME GRANDFATHER OF THE NATION MUST HAVE BEEN DELIGHTFUL."

it became abundantly clear there was no way Bill could stay, and how they tried to get him out of the show early. He was pretty devastated, but I think he understood. The incredibly sad thing about that recently discovered interview with Bill [which appears on the *Tenth Planet* DVD] is that he talks about making a success in another part, but I think you can see in his eyes that he knows that's not going to happen. He was raging against the dying of the light, I suppose."

The role of William Hartnell is played by David Bradley, an actor who, at 71, is close to the age Hartnell was trying to evoke on screen. The inspiration to cast Bradley came from an unlikely source.

"I mentioned the idea to [*Shaun of the Dead* director] Edgar Wright eight years ago, and he was the one who suggested David," says Gatiss. "I'd previously considered a few people who had a physical resemblance to Hartnell. It was obviously more important to get someone terrific, but a physical resemblance was a good way in. As soon as Edgar mentioned David I thought he was absolutely perfect.

"There is a redemptive quality to this, much like *A Christmas Carol*, which happens to be my favourite story. I think to play a successful Scrooge you have to be an inherently nice person who can play nasty very well. I don't think you can be a nasty

Above: David Bradley as William Hartnell in *An Adventure in Space and Time*.

Top right: One of Hartnell's final scenes, with Michael Craze and Anneke Wills, in Episode 4 of *The Tenth Planet* (1966).

Right: A February 1963 publicity shot of Carole Ann Ford. Later that year Ford was cast as the Doctor's granddaughter Susan.

person and then play his redemption. David has spent most of his life playing baddies, but he is the nicest man in the world. David admires Bill Hartnell very much, and I think he really got to the heart of this cantankerous old actor."

In what way did playing Doctor Who redeem Hartnell?

"There's a scene where Bill is trying to explain to his granddaughter what he's doing. He says, 'I play a funny old man who lives in a magic box. He's called the Doctor.' Little Judith says, 'Does he make people better?' And in fact that's just what he does, and that's what he did for Bill.

"Totally unexpectedly he became a hero to children. That's an incredible thing for anyone to cope with, especially for someone like Bill, who had become prematurely old and very bad-tempered. There's some wonderful Super 8 footage of him attending an air show, dressed as the Doctor. It makes your heart melt because you can see how much he loved it. For Bill Hartnell, to have become the grandfather of the nation must have been delightful. This is something about the character that continues to this day – if you're the Doctor you can just step into the room and children's faces light up."

To help Bradley prepare for the role, Gatiss bought him the DVD box-set containing the first three stories and showed him the recently discovered filmed interview with Hartnell.

"That came along at just the right time," says Gatiss. "If it wasn't for that we wouldn't have had much to go on except a transcript of Bill's *Desert Island Discs*! The interview was filmed in 1967; he's only just left the show and he looks like he's got

the weight of the world on his shoulders. It's the whole story in two minutes, and that was perfect for David."

There is a consensus that the character of the Doctor we recognise from more recent portrayals had its roots in Patrick Troughton's interpretation. If so, where does that leave Hartnell?

"It's easy for people to dismiss Bill as a doddery old fool who couldn't remember his lines," replies Gatiss, "and to say that everything was okay once Troughton started. But the show was *incredibly* successful when Bill starred in it, and to a whole generation he is still the definitive Doctor. The more I watch his episodes the fonder I become of his characterisation, and when you see the 1967 interview you realise how much of a characterisation it was. Bill Hartnell is not the Doctor the way that Jon Pertwee was the Doctor, for example. He was not playing himself."

What would Hartnell have made of the fact that the BBC has celebrated his life – and one of his greatest achievements – in this new film?

"I think Bill would be chuffed to bits to know that *Doctor Who* was still going strong 50 years later," says Gatiss. "William Russell [who played Ian Chesterton in the first two series] was one of the people I interviewed when I was working on the script. I asked him how Bill would've felt about a film being made of his life.

"He said, 'I'll tell you what he would have liked the most. He's on a bloody stamp!'" ✳

BEING FIRST

David Bradley discusses his meticulous preparation for playing
William Hartnell in *An Adventure in Space and Time*.

INTERVIEW BY **SIMON GUERRIER**

"**O**ne day, I shall come back..."

Fifty years after he first appeared on our screens, the original incarnation of the Doctor is back on BBC Television, returning to the same junkyard on Totter's Lane where we first met him. *An Adventure in Space and Time* tells the story of *Doctor Who*'s early years, with David Bradley cast as William Hartnell.

Bradley was first offered the role of William Hartnell on 3 June 2012 while on the roof of the National Theatre in London. He was there to watch the Queen's Diamond Jubilee flotilla as it passed down the Thames. Mark Gatiss was also present. "I'd met Mark briefly in Covent Garden six, seven years ago," he recalls. "I was getting off the 73 bus and he stopped and said hello. But

we'd never worked together or anything. So it was a bit out of the blue when he asked if I'd be interested in doing this."

The BBC's press release announcing the drama quoted Bradley as saying "I almost bit his hand off!" He laughs at that now. "Yes, I knew straight away, with it being in Mark's hands. I'd seen some of his stuff, not only *The League of Gentlemen* but his *Sherlock* series, and I knew he was a terrific writer. And he made it quite clear how passionate he was about the subject and how he'd always wanted to do this. So I didn't even think to ask if I could see a script or anything. I just said 'Yes, please, when do we start?'"

For Bradley, researching the role meant watching lots and lots of old *Doctor Who*. "Mark sent me a box-set of the first few stories," he says, "and the version of the first episode that had to be remade. And there was stuff on YouTube, little out-takes and things like that. There was lots of material to work from, but that of course was for the character of the Doctor. There's little record of William Hartnell as he was in real life."

Bradley was able to see a newly discovered clip of Hartnell promoting a pantomime soon after he'd left *Doctor Who*; the clip has subsequently been included on the DVD release of *The Tenth Planet*. But it's only a brief glimpse of the man. "Otherwise," says Bradley, "all we've got are his films. Of course, I'd already seen *The Way Ahead*, *This Sporting Life* and *Brighton Rock*.

"He was one of those brilliant British character actors," he adds. "He was maybe ahead of his time in terms of naturalness – his power and sheer charisma on screen. He played a lot of authority figures. Sergeant majors and rather stiff, domineering characters. In *The Army Game* he was the only one not getting laughs. And he was getting tired of that. He wanted to show that he could do comedy and light-hearted stuff." ▶

COMEDIC ROLES

Although Hartnell's film career is defined by a number of intense dramatic roles, David Bradley soon became aware that he was also adept at comedy. "I read some reviews of his early performances on stage, before he hit the screen," he says. "By all accounts he was a brilliant farceur, very funny and a great mimic. Just from watching his films you wouldn't know that. So watching him in *Doctor Who*,

doing something a bit more whimsical, sensitive and light-hearted, made me realise how versatile he was.

"He could be quite cruel as the Doctor, and quite cunning and manipulative, but he could also be quite impish and had a sense of curiosity about the universe and everything in it. And I could see, as an actor, that he was having fun. I think it was the best thing that ever happened to him, really."

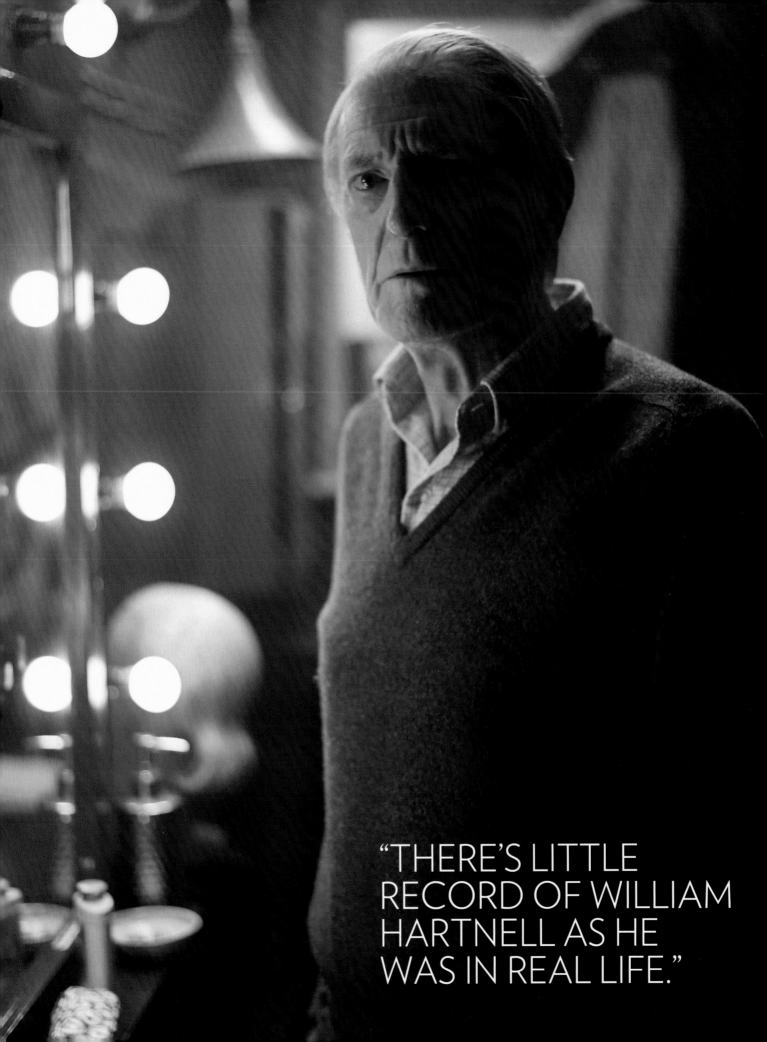

"THERE'S LITTLE RECORD OF WILLIAM HARTNELL AS HE WAS IN REAL LIFE."

OTHER DOCTORS

PETER CUSHING
(*DR. WHO AND THE DALEKS, DALEKS' INVASION EARTH 2150 A.D.*)

Cushing was an international star in Hammer's legendary horror films when he took the role of Dr Who in two big-screen movies released in the mid-1960s. Knowing that children would adore the films, and eager to take his work in a new direction, Cushing embraced the potential for comedy in the part but nevertheless showed occasional flashes of steely determination.

TREVOR MARTIN
(*SEVEN KEYS TO DOOMSDAY*)

Martin played a Time Lord in *The War Games* in 1969 and was cast as the Doctor in the 1974 stage production *Seven Keys to Doomsday*. He won the approval of author Terrance Dicks, but the play sadly never got beyond its original West End engagement. Since then, Martin has worked regularly on TV (recently in *Whitechapel* and *Call the Midwife*) and in films including *The House of Mirth* and *Babel*.

RICHARD HURNDALL
(*THE FIVE DOCTORS*)

Stage and TV veteran Hurndall was chosen to play the First Doctor in 1983's *The Five Doctors*, his similarity to William Hartnell noted when he appeared as the elderly slave Nebrox in *Blake's 7*. At home in comedy or high drama, Hurndall's credits range from *War and Peace* to *Steptoe and Son*.

RICHARD E GRANT
(*SCREAM OF THE SHALKA*)

Best known for his dissipated turn as Withnail in *Withnail and I* opposite Paul McGann, Grant played the Doctor in the 2003 animated webcast *Scream of the Shalka*. In 1995, he starred in *Franz Kafka's It's A Wonderful Life*, the Oscar–winning short film directed by Peter Capaldi. More recently Grant appeared in *Doctor Who* as Dr Simeon, puppet of the Great Intelligence.

As an experienced screen actor, what struck Bradley most while watching the early episodes of *Doctor Who* was how hard it must have been on the actors. "You had to do a whole scene in one fell swoop, without any breaks. If, under that pressure, an actor forgot his lines the camera had to keep rolling so it was virtually like live television. I should imagine it was quite nerve-wracking and tense. But, watching the episodes now, the way they handled it is so cool and professional." He laughs. "Nowadays we have it easy, really. If I blow a line I just stop and the director will say 'Okay, let's pick it up from the line before.'"

That means Bradley is sympathetic to Hartnell's occasional slips. "There are clips on YouTube where Bill has totally lost it and is struggling for his lines," he says. "William Russell [playing companion Ian] is leaning in, trying to give him a clue. It's kind of funny but also grim viewing because you know that this guy's a perfectionist and demands a lot of himself. He's struggling to maintain his own professional standards. It just makes him terribly human."

Top: David Bradley as William Hartnell and Lesley Manville as Hartnell's wife Heather in *An Adventure in Space and Time*.

Centre: Hartnell with Heather and their daughter Anne (left) at the première of *Brighton Rock* in 1947.

Above: Jessica Carney's 1996 biography of her grandfather.

Right: Hartnell, William Russell and Carole Ann Ford rehearse *The Aztecs* in May 1964.

What really helped Bradley understand Hartnell was the biography, *Who's There*, written by Hartnell's granddaughter Jessica Carney. "She gave me a copy to read," he says. "I was just amazed at his early life and his difficulties. He very nearly took to street crime and for a while was a bit of an urchin. There were the difficulties he had because of his illegitimacy, which nowadays we don't even think about – it might even help you get a book deal! But back then the stigma attached to it was such that he suffered quite a lot, at school particularly. So I was just finding out stuff about his life, which helped me get an insight into why he was as he was."

It also helped that, at the first read-through of *An Adventure in Space and Time* and again during recording, the actors and crew who'd known and worked with Hartnell were on hand to give advice. "It was a joy watching their faces as they walked through the studio, seeing the set as it had been 50 years ago," Bradley remembers.

"The first shot I did was me walking away from the camera on the way to the TARDIS for the last time. It was just a low tracking shot of my feet and the cloak flapping. Waris Hussein, the original director, was watching that on the monitor, as he would have been 50 years ago. Mark was standing alongside him and saw the tears rolling down his cheeks."

Bradley admits, however, that he was also a bit daunted by having the original cast and crew around. "I just thought, 'Wow!' Because the responsibility of playing this man suddenly hit me. It helped, having them there, and thankfully they all gave me the thumbs up and were very encouraging and positive. I could wander up to William Russell and say, 'What was he like after a few drinks?' It was a real bonus.

FIRST AND TWELFTH

Many members of *Doctor Who*'s original cast and crew visited the set of *An Adventure in Space and Time* – but there was also a visit from the show's future. "I'd never met Peter Capaldi [pictured] before, only admired him from afar," says Bradley. "We chatted for a while and he watched a scene and was very complimentary about what we did. He revealed that he'd been a huge *Doctor Who* fan all his life. That's why he came along, just out of interest. I don't think he knew he was going to be the Doctor then, but now I'm thinking back I wonder if

he'd been given the tip-off? I didn't know. It was a huge surprise – a happy one – when he got that gig. He'll be terrific."

OTHER DOCTORS

MICHAEL JAYSTON

(*THE TRIAL OF A TIME LORD*)
After worldwide acclaim for his portrayal of the doomed Tsar Nicholas in the 1971 epic *Nicholas and Alexandra* (co-starring with Tom Baker as Rasputin) Jayston was constantly in demand as an actor and voice artist. In 1986 he brought particular relish to his role as the Valeyard, a malevolent entity "from the darker side of the Doctor's nature, somewhere between his 12th and final incarnation."

ROWAN ATKINSON

(*THE CURSE OF FATAL DEATH*)
In Steven Moffat's Comic Relief extravaganza of 1999, *Blackadder* and *Mr Bean* star Atkinson was a note-perfect Doctor, with Julia Sawalha as his assistant Emma. At the finale Richard E Grant, Jim Broadbent, Hugh Grant and Joanna Lumley played further incarnations in rapid succession.

TOBY JONES

(*AMY'S CHOICE*)
In 2010 Jones played the Dream Lord, a twisted reflection of the Doctor manifested in the TARDIS by hallucinogenic spores. The actor is following in the footsteps of his famous father, Freddie Jones, and is fast becoming one of Britain's premier character players. He was outstanding as Truman Capote in *Infamous* (2006), and has more recently been seen in *Tinker Tailor Soldier Spy* and *Berberian Sound Studio*.

JOHN HURT
(*THE NAME OF THE DOCTOR, THE DAY OF THE DOCTOR*)
An unassuming movie star, Hurt came to fame in the late 1970s with meticulous performances in *The Naked Civil Servant*, *Alien* and *The Elephant Man*. His surprise appearance in the closing moments of *The Name of the Doctor* set up an intriguing anniversary conundrum for all *Doctor Who* fans.

David Miller

Above: Bradley at the controls of the TARDIS, with Claudia Grant as Carole Ann Ford/Susan.

Below: Brian Cox plays Sydney Newman, *Doctor Who's* co-creator, in *An Adventure in Space and Time.*

"But the biggest bonus was of course Mark's wonderful script. It shows a lot of different sides to Bill; it doesn't try to soften or sentimentalise him in any way. It's just a brilliant piece of astute character writing. Playing someone as complex as Hartnell was – and he certainly was, he had many different sides to him – is pure gold for an actor.

"Three and a half weeks' of filming isn't really long for a 90-minute drama," Bradley adds, "but it seemed to go without any huge hitches. I didn't feel any pressure in that sense. I just felt a responsibility to do justice to the man and the actor. Hopefully, we've done that.

"Of course," he concludes, "we've made this for the fans but also we hope it stands up on its own for people who've never seen an episode of *Doctor Who* but are interested in a good human drama. It's quite a story really; the start of *Doctor Who* was fraught with difficulties and very nearly didn't happen. Hopefully this drama will stand as a testament to Verity Lambert and Sydney Newman (*Doctor Who's* original producer and creator) as well as Hartnell. The three of them, they're huge heroes in this story, sticking to their guns like they did. They left us with 50 years of a cultural phenomenon."

So, if asked, would Bradley play the First Doctor again, perhaps looking in on his latest incarnation in the TV series itself? "Well, that *is* a question! It hasn't come up but it's a very tempting thought…" He considers. "If someone was to suggest it, I'd certainly be interested, yes." ✳

PATRICK TROUGHTON

The restless career and tangled private life of the man who gave *Doctor Who* a second chance.

FEATURE BY **JONATHAN RIGBY**

His was one of the truly great television faces. The furrowed brow, the hooded eyes, the narrow upper lip, the deep seams running down from the nose… It was a face that could slip imperceptibly from the clownish to the demonic, making him ideal for the ambiguous title role in *Doctor Who*.

Yet it was this distinctive face that Patrick Troughton felt a near-obsessive need to conceal. He believed that a true character actor should maintain his anonymity at all times, and for this reason the offer to play the Doctor conjured up his greatest fear – typecasting.

The offer came through in July 1966. Troughton was in County Wicklow at the time, making *The Viking Queen* for Hammer Films. At first he thought it absurd; after all, continuing a popular series through the expedient of the title character literally changing his face was a revolutionary concept at the time. He was convinced it would kill *Doctor Who* stone dead. Not only that, he was convinced it would kill his career stone dead.

But, with half a dozen children to support, he duly signed up on Tuesday 2 August. Next, he started sketching out (literally) various character ideas. Remembering WC Fields in *Mississippi*, he fancied himself as a 19th-century steamboat skipper. Remembering Conrad Veidt in *The Thief of Bagdad*,

he determined to 'black up' and wear a turban. Remembering himself in the 1950 Disney version of *Treasure Island*, he thought a grizzled, eyepatch-wearing pirate might do the trick. These and several other disguises, he told his sons David and Michael, were conceived on the principle that "I don't want anyone to know 'who' is playing Who."

Indeed, just moments before shooting his first scene in *The Power of the Daleks* on 22 October, he was still wearing a crazily curled wig that, to the Doctor's current companions, was unacceptably reminiscent of Harpo Marx. Playfully but firmly, Michael Craze and Anneke Wills refused to act with him if he continued to wear it. The last-minute solution was a mop-top 'do' suggesting a rather more modish figure – Ringo Starr.

These uncertainties (among them, a rapidly discarded Paris Beau hat) continued for a while even after Troughton's Doctor made his television début. By his own admission, he had to gradually 'dial down' his eccentric performance in the course of his initial stories. "After a rather stop-start beginning while the audience wondered who the heck that was taking over," he told interviewer John Peel 20 years later, "they settled down and started to like me."

Troughton's triumph in the role was crucial to the success of *Doctor Who* at a particularly precarious time. For not only did his 'cosmic hobo' persona – superficially skittish but profoundly wise – constitute a decisive break with William Hartnell's professorial characterisation. It also ensured the ▶

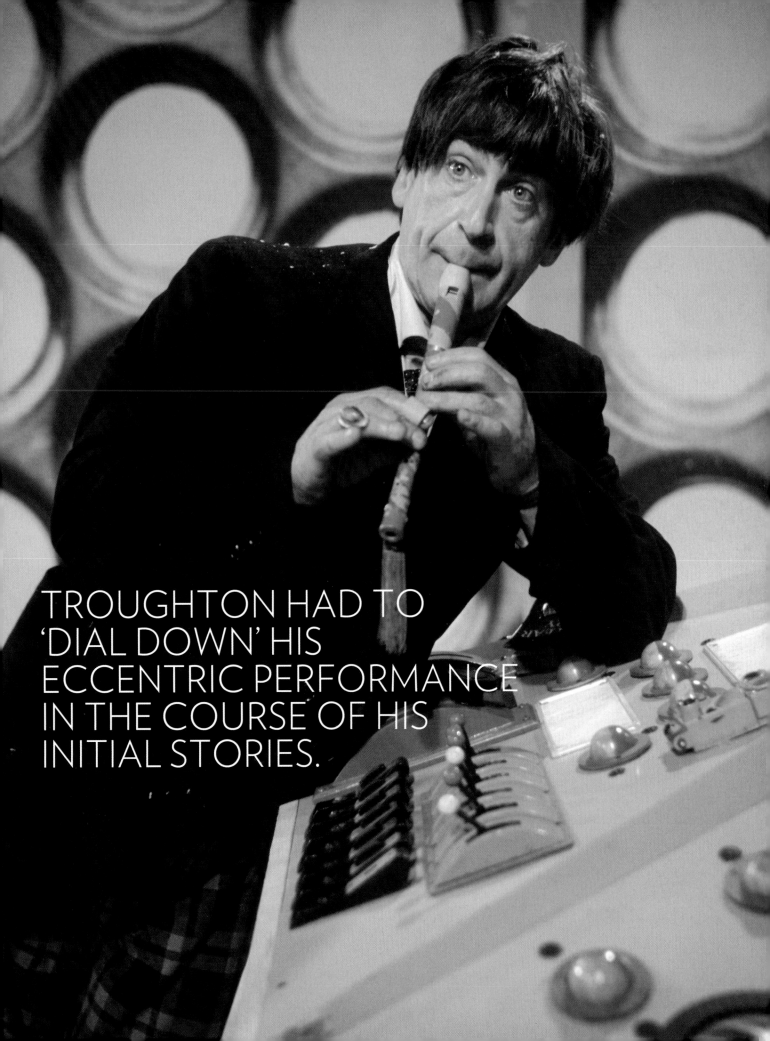

TROUGHTON HAD TO
'DIAL DOWN' HIS
ECCENTRIC PERFORMANCE
IN THE COURSE OF HIS
INITIAL STORIES.

> ## "I REMEMBER THE PART JUST OVERWHELMING ME, MAKING ME INCONSISTENT AND ARGUMENTATIVE."

Top: A publicity shot taken during the recording of *The War Games* on 12 June 1969 – Troughton's final day as the Doctor until he returned to the role in 1972.

Top right: Rehearsing his lines during the Welsh location filming for *The Abominable Snowmen* in September 1967.

Above: As Salamander, the Doctor's doppelgänger, in *The Enemy of the World* (1967-68).

Right: As *Paul of Tarsus* in the BBC serial of 1960.

longevity of a show that might otherwise have imploded just three years after it began.

Born in Mill Hill on 25 March 1920, Troughton trained as an actor in both London and New York. Having ended the war in command of a North Sea gunboat, he then joined the Bristol Old Vic prior to making his film and TV débuts in 1947 – as the Player King in Olivier's *Hamlet*, then immediately afterwards as Horatio in a BBC production of the same play.

He soon decided that TV was the route to at least a measure of financial security. With only occasional exceptions (such as an Olivier rep season on Broadway in 1952), he would ignore theatre thereafter and focus on BBC title roles like *Robin Hood* (TV's first, in 1953) and *Paul of Tarsus* (1960), together with Quilp in *The Old Curiosity Shop* (1962) and Dr Manette in *A Tale of Two Cities* (1965).

Financial security was of particular importance to an actor whose private life was more tangled than most. He maintained two families; the first, begun in 1947, was domiciled in Mill Hill and the second, begun ten years later, in Kew. Yet when he finally divorced his first wife in the mid-1970s, he married not the mother of his second family, but a close friend of hers. His eldest daughter, Joanna, never spoke to him again.

These details of Troughton's double life were kept firmly under wraps because by that time *Doctor Who* had made him a national figure. Perhaps it's significant that, among his 21 stories, Troughton particularly relished the chance to play his own double in *The Enemy of the World*. This story fell right in the middle of what he delightedly called "the year of my monsters," a Season Five purple patch in which the Doctor faced Ice Warriors, Cybermen (twice), robotic Yeti (ditto) and sentient seaweed in rapid succession. He also valued the camaraderie he shared with companions Frazer Hines, Deborah Watling and Wendy Padbury, describing his *Doctor Who* period as "the three best years of my life."

But there was a downside. "It was weekly rep," he lamented in 1986. "We had two and a half days to do it and then you were on. We had four weeks in the summer, in August, when we could go on holiday and so on. But it was very hard work. You were like a squirrel on a wheel."

So much so that his co-workers couldn't help noticing how the effervescent practical joker of Troughton's first two years in the role was replaced in the third by a tetchy and visibly exhausted leading man. "Towards the end I began to care too much," he confided to his son Michael. "Most of all, I didn't want to be responsible for killing off *Who*. I remember the part just overwhelming me, making me inconsistent and argumentative. Almost schizophrenic."

This, coupled with his continuing horror of typecasting, compelled him in January 1969 to announce his retirement from *Doctor Who*. To his amazement, a week before recording his final scenes in June of that year he was offered a major role in the lavish BBC serial *The Six Wives of Henry VIII*. This was just the first of a flood of offers, making his

OTHER ROLES

THE OLD CURIOSITY SHOP (1962)
Troughton's dwarfish Daniel Quilp entailed almost back-breaking contortions and brought him rave reviews. An opportunity in 1979 to repeat the role (again for the BBC) was curtailed by his first heart attack; Trevor Peacock played it instead.

JASON AND THE ARGONAUTS (1963)
Troughton's scenes as the blind and tormented Phineus (filmed near Sorrento) involved him in a classic encounter with Ray Harryhausen's animated harpies.

SCARS OF DRACULA (1970)
Troughton made several Hammer horrors; this was by no means the best, but his Klove (masochistic minion to Christopher Lee) was an over-ripe delight. Furthermore, his make-up is a direct repeat of his Quilp look.

THE OMEN (1976)
Steeped in sin and guilt, Troughton's demented Father Brennan in this Satanic smash is extraordinary – he really makes you believe that Brennan has encountered spiritual evil. His climactic impalement by a church lightning conductor is justly famous.

A HITCH IN TIME (1978)
This slightly cut-price Children's Film Foundation featurette is intriguing for Troughton's role as Adam Wagstaff, an eccentric, mutton-chopped inventor who just happens to have created a time machine.

THE BOX OF DELIGHTS (1984)
After his second heart scare, Troughton went straight into this classic six-part adaptation of the John Masefield novel; the bearded magus Cole Hawlings remains arguably his most enduring latterday performance.

typecasting worries seem ridiculous. As a result, he was happy to make fleeting returns to *Doctor Who* in 1973 (*The Three Doctors*), 1983 (*The Five Doctors*) and 1985 (*The Two Doctors*).

By the mid-1980s, Troughton had relaxed his former resistance to talking about the show; one thing he wouldn't relax, against his doctor's advice, was his stressful work-load. These two factors crossed over with fatal consequences in March 1987 when, straight after his 67th birthday, he was a guest at Magnum Opus Con II in Columbus, Georgia.

On the afternoon of Friday the 27th he regaled the assembled *Who* fans with his plans for his latest role, Lord Steyne in a BBC serialisation of *Vanity Fair*. He envisaged red whiskers, buck teeth, an unblinking gaze, and even tried out the plummy voice he had in mind. But early the following morning he died of a heart attack in his hotel bedroom – bequeathing Lord Steyne, as it turned out, to the much younger John Shrapnel.

With his death, British television lost one of its most intriguing actors, a man who placed a high value on the chameleon mutability that allowed him to create a broad range of characters. While this constant desire for change enriched his performances, the same compulsion in his private life brought confusion to his partners and children.

Indeed, his son Michael has singled out one of the Second Doctor's very first pronouncements as a line that could have been written by Troughton himself. Assessing his newly transformed appearance the Doctor has a philosophical explanation ready for his incredulous companions.

"Life," he tells them, "depends on change. And renewal." ✳

Top: Douglas Camfield (left) directs Troughton and Frazer Hines in location filming for *The Invasion* (1968).

Above: A signed publicity postcard from *The Five Doctors* (1983).

SCRIPTING THE SECOND DOCTOR

This was an era of clearly defined – and often confined – threats.

FEATURE BY **JUSTIN RICHARDS**

The archetypal Second Doctor narrative is perhaps easier to codify than others. Simply put, almost every story in this era pits the Doctor against a distinct – and distinctive – threat, with the threat usually being alluded to in the story's title. Indeed, with the sole exception of 1968's *Fury from the Deep*, the title of every Second Doctor story starts with 'The' something or other, emphasising that threat.

Monsters are the key component that sets the Second Doctor's era apart. Only a handful of stories don't feature a monstrous enemy, and unless the threat is notable for some other reason – like the appearance of the Doctor's double in *The Enemy of the World* (1967-68) or the parallels between the aliens and the Doctor's own people in *The War Games* (1969) – these monster-free stories are less successful. The fact that the 'monsters' in *The Underwater Menace* (1967) don't actually constitute the advertised 'menace' certainly counts against it.

When the Second Doctor battles monsters he does so, almost always, in a closed environment.

THIS IS A DOCTOR WHO ISN'T AFRAID TO RUN AWAY WHEN DISCRETION IS THE BETTER PART OF VALOUR.

It's not quite the generic 'base under siege' situation, but even the epic scope of *The War Games* is stretched across a landscape that can be drawn on a simple map. Frequently, as in *The Moonbase* (1967) and *The Wheel in Space* (1968), the settings offer no escape and to a large extent define the stories themselves – and provide their titles.

Even when the canvas seems broader, it's still restricted. *The Evil of the Daleks* (1967) narrows from contemporary London to Maxtible's country estate then to the Dalek City on Skaro; *The War Games* from various battlefields to the aliens' HQ to a courtroom on the Doctor's home planet. Similarly, *The Abominable Snowmen* and *The Ice Warriors* (both 1967) are set in theoretically vast landscapes but actually confined to a handful of linked locations. Only *The Highlanders* (1966-7), *The Enemy of the World*, *The Invasion* (1968) and *The Space Pirates* (1969) explore a wider landscape.

The programme's limited access to location filming in this era underpins the claustrophobic backdrop to so many stories – be it the Tube tunnels of *The Web of Fear* (1968), the titular *Tomb of the Cybermen* (1967) or the isolated industrial complexes of *Fury from the Deep*. As well as making a narrative strength out of a production weakness,

the use of confined locations also emphasises the threat – and size – of the monsters.

Of course, the threat is only as great as the conviction of the actors can make it. We remember Patrick Troughton's Second Doctor as something of a clown but, in those expertly judged moments when he's serious, he engenders a real sense of fear and peril. "There are some corners of the universe which have bred the most terrible things," he says. And from the way he says it, the way the clown becomes the doomsayer, we believe him.

This is a Doctor who isn't afraid to run away when discretion is the better part of valour. "When I say run, run," is a phrase that crops up multiple times. But that doesn't mean the Doctor is abandoning his friends, or hope. As often as not he runs straight *into* trouble rather than away from it. In *The Tomb of the Cybermen*, the Doctor is instrumental in reactivating the Cyber equipment – perhaps realising that it's better to force a confrontation while he's on hand to deal with it rather than delay the Cybermen's inevitable re-awakening.

An earlier Cyber-story, the First Doctor's final serial *The Tenth Planet* (1966), seems to present a prototype for the typical Second Doctor adventure, but it does so only in terms of the

confined setting. The Doctor's presence in *The Tenth Planet* is incidental. The Second Doctor may lurk in the background but he's always central to the battle and instrumental in the monsters' eventual defeat.

So there it is – the typical Second Doctor story is set in a confined environment that the monsters have already started to infiltrate, little realising that the diminutive, clownish figure earning the trust of the besieged community has a notion of how to defeat them... ✳

A HAPPY SORT OF PART

Notoriously publicity-shy during the 1960s, Patrick Troughton only discovered the depth of affection towards his Doctor when he started attending conventions much later. These interviews capture him in affable spirits.

FEATURE BY **SIMON GUERRIER**

On Saturday 21 March 1986, the Highway Hotel in Concorde, New Hampshire hosted the *Doctor Who* Festival and Exhibit Tour. Fans paid $12 (or $15 for reserved seats at the front) to watch *The Two Doctors* ahead of its broadcast on Channel 11. They also got to meet the Second Doctor.

For an hour, actor Patrick Troughton discussed his time as the Doctor and his career more generally. Jeff Lyons, then a journalist for WCFR Radio, recorded the whole thing. Troughton was softly spoken, slightly posher than he sounded as the Doctor and very good at encouraging nervous fans to ask questions. He was also surprisingly well briefed.

At the time, *Doctor Who* had been off the air in the UK for a year – the longest break in its history at that point – and there were rumours in the press suggesting it might never return.

"*The Times* got it wrong," Troughton insisted. "They start making this new lot [*The Trial of a Time Lord*] in a week. There's going to be a thread right the way through – the stories are linked in some way."

Rewinding to his own time, Troughton pointed out that, after he left the series in 1969, *Doctor Who* dropped from 40 episodes a year to a mere 25. "I don't remember any sort of outcry at that. Mind you, old Pertwee was probably very pleased at [getting] a bit of a break."

Asked if the Doctor is a good part, Troughton promptly replied, "Not half. Actors get very possessive about it. Colin [Baker, the then-current Doctor] wants to go on forever." But he was candid about his own uncertainties while playing the role. Before being asked to take over from William Hartnell, he'd watched the series with his young children and had decided views. "After three years with Billy, it was getting played out. Some of the stories were a bit thin. And I just didn't see myself in the part."

Why not? "I had no idea how to play it. I knew they didn't want an imitation of Billy but I was completely nonplussed." So what convinced him? "They wooed me over a week, the money went up every day, and then I said yes," he laughed. ▶

Opposite page: In late 1967 Patrick Troughton revealed the winning entries in *Blue Peter's* 'Design a Monster' competition. This was a rare personal appearance for the actor during the 1960s.

Above and right: 19 years later Troughton's attitude had softened. He is pictured here entertaining fans in New Jersey on 21 March 1986. Photos © Jeffrey Lyons.

Below: The Honey Monster – Troughton's inspiration for the fearsome Fred?

HONEY MONSTER

The *Doctor Who* Appreciation Society held its first convention in 1977, but Patrick Troughton didn't appear at one of its events until PanoptiCon VI in 1985. During his on-stage interview he was asked why he had stayed away for so long. "I didn't want to become too associated with the part again in this country," he explained. "In America that's different, because I don't appear over there except in repeats. I don't want to do it too much, just as I wouldn't want to do another *Who* for another two or three years if possible."

Troughton had clearly relished his recent appearance in *The Two Doctors*, and shared a proposal for a future adventure he had devised himself. "I've got a marvellous story which I want to put on one day about a little village which has been terrorised – rather like Dracula in Transylvania – by something which lives in the mountains. There's this awful aura of fear, and down comes the Doctor. He's very scared of this straight away, and he's persuaded much against his will to go and have a look. Towards the end of episode two he's walking and it's getting darker... he hears this hideous roaring noise in the distance. He keeps on going because he's very brave, and at the beginning of the next episode a smile comes on his face because he remembers that a great friend of his, called Fred, had a roar like that. A most hideous-looking creature, but the most lovable, warm-hearted creature in the universe. Anyhow they have a terrific party up in the mountains and then all the villagers come and try to get them!"

Troughton suggested that the villain in his none-too-serious story could resemble the Honey Monster from the Sugar Puffs television commercials.

MISSING EPISODES

"**R**eally, Jon Pertwee should have been after Billy [Hartnell] if they wanted a funny," said Patrick Troughton in 1985, "because Jon is, as you probably know, about the funniest man in the world. But coming after me, who it turned out became sort of funny, it spiked his guns a bit and he felt he wanted to play it straight. It seemed to me to be a waste of his wonderful talent."

Troughton was speaking at the PanoptiCon VI convention at the Brighton Metropole Hotel. The on-stage interview took him back to the day in 1966 when he was offered the role of the Doctor. He admitted that he had been a fan of the show since the first episode. "I had a young family in those days and we all watched," he said. "We were hooked for three years. I always enjoyed the ones which were futuristic, but not quite so much the ones which went back in time."

Conversation turned to the highlights of his own episodes, and a story which, at that time, was missing from the BBC's archive. "*The Tomb of the Cybermen* – that was a super one," he said. "A very good script and very frightening. They could do that one again, no problem with Colin [Baker]. He's a super Who."

He also remembered *The Enemy of the World*, a serial which at that time was largely missing. "It was rather fun really," he said, referring to playing both the Doctor and his doppelgänger Salamander. "It was difficult to believe in for me... to think, Can I do this and make the audience believe it? I don't know whether we did or not."

◄ "I thought, 'Even if it only lasts six weeks, it will be fantastic.' And here we are, 20 years later."

Elaborating on this theme, Troughton pointed out that "I wanted to relate to the younger members of the audience as well as the mums and dads. I knew the really small ones watched – and were scared stiff." One of Troughton's sons, aged six, was learning the recorder at school. "So he taught me to play a simple tune which all the schools were playing and I worked it into the first episode. Most directors after that tried to stop me doing it but I continued for a while and it seems to have stuck. I'd love to be able to play an instrument. If I work hard at the recorder it's not too bad."

Troughton's children were "tickled pink" when he got the part, though by then they were used to seeing their father on television. "It was lovely playing the Doctor with a young family growing up. Being a very happy sort of part, you carry that home with you." Not everyone was so impressed, however. "My wife of that time was not a great television viewer. She loved ballet and live theatre. I confess that she was delighted more for the family because it was regular work for me and meant we could educate the children privately on the proceeds."

Again, he was surprisingly candid at this point. "I had two families at that time. You tend to say, 'Oh, thank you very much. Yes, I want to work.'"

Despite his doubts, Troughton settled quickly into playing the Doctor and was a huge success. But the majority of his episodes no longer exist in the BBC archive. "I'm livid. I'd love them all to have survived. But I believe there are whole lots all over the world which fans are keeping close, which we hope one day will come to light."

Inevitably, the questions from the audience concentrated on those stories that do exist and which fans had watched. Troughton picked a favourite. "*The Mind Robber* was a very ingenious story. I had a lot to do in it, in the midst of a very hard schedule. It was worth it, although we grumbled a lot at the time. You see, one was working at such a pitch... You didn't really have time to say 'This is a good one' or 'This is a bad one.' Television is a monster and has to be fed, nearly 24 hours of the day now. It's a nice monster, though."

Troughton was a little sheepish when asked if he watched his old episodes. "Er, yes I do," he admitted. "I've got one video – *The Seeds of Death*. To watch me 20 years ago is quite an education, because I'm that much quicker mentally in the part. I wish that tape had been available before I tackled the *Three* or *Five* or *Two Doctors* because you can't resurrect the part exactly. And also there's the scripts." When Troughton was in the series full-time, he explained, "Obviously all the

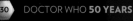

writers were writing particularly for me, so it fell into a pattern and was easier to act."

Of his three returns to the role, *The Two Doctors* was the easiest because Frazer Hines was also returning as companion Jamie. "It was extraordinary," Troughton pointed out. "The years just fell away. Looking at it, I'm a little slower and greyer but it was lovely." He was also full of praise for Colin Baker, "who is absolutely super. Colin and I are on the same wavelength… I enjoy working with him very much indeed."

Would he return to *Doctor Who*, a fan asked, for its 25th anniversary in 1988? "If we all joined in, of course I would. Whenever I'm asked, I'd love to." But would he want to come back more permanently, say, if Baker left the series? "I think that would be a mistake. I like to pop up perhaps once every two years, ideally. Not more than that

"TELEVISION IS A MONSTER AND IT HAS TO BE FED, NEARLY 24 HOURS OF THE DAY NOW. IT'S A NICE MONSTER, THOUGH."

because I've got to make my living as a character actor… And I don't think I'd be asked to come back." He laughs. "It will probably be an African lady next – or eventually. Or a Chinese lady. That'd be fun."

Troughton had just a year to live at the time of the interview but, judging from the tape, he was still full of life, relishing the prospect of new work and new challenges. Having explained that he didn't like acting on stage, he added, "I wouldn't mind doing farce. I was offered a part in *A Funny Thing Happened on the Way to the Forum* at Chichester this year, but it clashed with the situation comedy [ITV's *The Two of Us*]. If it had been in London I might just have done both.

"It would be nice to hear an audience and have the clapping afterwards. I haven't had that for about 40 years. In television you do the show, have a drink afterwards, say goodbye to everyone and go home. That's why I love coming here," he concluded. "You actually hear that somebody liked you." ✳

Opposite page top left: *The Tomb of the Cybermen* (1967).

Opposite page top right: A camera rehearsal for one of Troughton's favourite stories, *The Mind Robber* (1968).

Opposite page centre: Answering fans' questions in New Jersey. Photo © Jeffrey Lyons.

Opposite page below: A split personality in *The Enemy of the World* (1967-68).

Above left: *The Two Doctors* (1985) featured Troughton's final performance in the role.

Above right: In relaxed mood at New Jersey. Photos © Jeffrey Lyons.

Right: Flute for thought in *Fury from the Deep* (1968).

JON PERTWEE

The casting of the Third Doctor was part of the programme's greatest transformation, and the beginning of a journey of self-discovery for actor Jon Pertwee.

FEATURE BY **JONATHAN RIGBY**

Above: Jon Pertwee acts the clown – if not yet the dandy – during his first *Doctor Who* photocall on 17 June 1969.

Opposite page: On location at Peckforton Castle, Cheshire, for *The Time Warrior* in May 1973.

Below: A publicity shot taken during the location filming of *Spearhead from Space* in Ealing on 19 September 1969.

Below right: With Nicholas Courtney (as the Brigadier) during the filming of *Doctor Who and the Silurians* at Hankley Common, Surrey, on 17 November 1969.

Whenever he was asked about his preference for earthbound *Doctor Who* adventures, Jon Pertwee had a well-rehearsed answer ready. As befitted the man, it was structured as a joke but concealed a profound insight. "I've always said that there's nothing more alarming than coming home and finding a Yeti sitting on your loo in Tooting Bec," he claimed in 1984.

That Pertwee understood this basic principle – that horror works best when the abnormal intrudes into the normal – was just as well. For not only did his early *Who* stories confine the Doctor to 1970s Earth, they also triggered controversy about the show's increasingly disturbing content. Bestriding a chamber of horrors that included homicidal mannequins, faceless astronauts and animated gargoyles, all of them located in workaday surroundings, the debonair Pertwee proved himself a delightfully reassuring presence.

"The newest recruit is suave and confident: obviously a Harley Street doctor," mused the *Daily Mirror*'s Matthew Coady when Pertwee's first story, *Spearhead from Space*, appeared in January 1970. "At the same time he manages to look like Danny Kaye while sounding like Boris Karloff – and that's a mixture for the connoisseur."

This reconceived Doctor was clearly something of a connoisseur himself, a dandified James Bond in velvety Edwardian threads with a pronounced taste for action and adventure. Yet at first Pertwee was uncertain.

He'd been hired with a view to building up the comic touches that Patrick Troughton had brought to the Second Doctor; Pertwee, after all, was known almost exclusively as a comic actor. So for his first couple of episodes he was lumbered with a few bits of semi-farcical business that dismayed him, for his impulse was to play it straight. In following his instincts he made a remarkable discovery.

"We both of us hid under what we called a green umbrella," he once said. "We never allowed our own personalities to come through." He was speaking of his friend Peter Sellers, whose galaxy of comic grotesques vied with his own. Yet, when cast in *Doctor Who* in 1969, Pertwee was asked by Head of Drama Shaun Sutton to just play 'Jon Pertwee'. "Who the hell's that?" he wondered. ▶

IN CRAFTING
THE THIRD
DOCTOR, HE
REALISED
THAT 'PERTWEE'
WASN'T THE
COMIC ZANY
HE WAS
FAMOUS
FOR.

"THE CLOAK WAS MY THING TO WRAP AROUND THE CHICKS TO PROTECT THEM. THE DOCTOR AS MOTHER HEN."

Top left: From 1955 to 1960 Pertwee was married to Jean Marsh, They are pictured here with their pet spaniel.

Top right: With Roger Delgado (as the Master), Katy Manning (as Jo Grant) and Nicholas Courtney (as the Brigadier) in a publicity shot from *Terror of the Autons* (1971).

Above: A portrait from the 1953 film *Will Any Gentleman...?*, in which Pertwee co-starred alongside William Hartnell.

Right: An EP taken from the 1962 comedy album *Jon Pertwee Sings Songs for Vulgar Boatmen*.

In crafting the Third Doctor, he realised that 'Pertwee' wasn't the comic zany he was famous for. He was more the heroic, compassionate, paternalistic man of action represented by the Doctor. "That's how I began to sort of discover myself," Pertwee confessed.

He was born in Chelsea, on 7 July 1919, with thespian leanings pretty much predetermined; his distinguished father, actor-playwright Roland Pertwee, was just the latest branch of a many-limbed theatrical family tree. Prefiguring a lifelong disdain for authoritarian stupidity, Pertwee Jr was expelled from numerous schools and even the Royal Academy of Dramatic Art. (He downed tools in no uncertain terms when given the absurdly fey assignment of enacting a 'wind'.) His first big break came at the Aldwych Theatre in June 1939, playing the juvenile lead in *To Kill a Cat*. He managed to get himself sacked from this too, despite the fact that the play was written by his father.

War service saw him playing a vital role in the Naval Intelligence Division, liaising with future James Bond author Ian Fleming and reporting directly to Winston Churchill. Post-war, he rapidly established himself as a major radio star, bringing his multifarious comic voices to series such as *Waterlogged Spa* and, pre-eminently, *The Navy Lark*. Films also came his way, including the 1953 comedy *Will Any Gentleman?* Working on this introduced him not only to future First Doctor William Hartnell but also the first Mrs Pertwee, actress Jean Marsh.

He enjoyed a couple of major West End hits in the 1960s, supporting Frankie Howerd in *A Funny Thing Happened on the Way to the Forum* and Donald Sinden in *There's a Girl in My*

Soup. In October 1967 the latter show took him to Broadway (this time supporting Gig Young), and it was during his lengthy spell at the Music Box Theatre that an offer came through regarding a new BBC sitcom called *Dad's Army*. He never regretted turning it down; as well as denying viewers Arthur Lowe's classic performance as Captain Mainwaring, he would have denied *himself* the opportunity to play the Third Doctor.

Prior to being cast, Pertwee had only caught two episodes of *Doctor Who*. The first he watched at the prompting of his ex-wife Jean, who in 1965 played Sara Kingdom in *The Daleks' Master Plan*. ("Bill [Hartnell] was tremendous in it," he told interviewers Matt Adams and David Southwell shortly before his death. "He remains my favourite Doctor.") Then came an episode of *The Web of Fear* in 1968. And that was it.

So he approached *Doctor Who* with very few preconceptions. In tandem with producer Barry Letts and script editor Terrance Dicks, he helped turn around a show whose viewing figures had dipped alarmingly in 1969. He did this in part by indulging aspects of his own, previously submerged, personality – an obsession with gadgets, a passion for speed (ranging all the way from the quaint Bessie to the super-smooth Whomobile), and a daredevil zeal for performing his own stunts.

Just as importantly, he fostered on set a family atmosphere that mirrored the close-knit UNIT community on screen. John Levene, who played the guileless Sergeant Benton, has gone so far as to say "Jon Pertwee was almost my surrogate father," while Katy Manning, cast as the effervescent Jo Grant, has made no secret of her adoration for her leading man.

Symbolic of Pertwee's centrality to this family 'unit' were his various Inverness capes, which on screen served a very special purpose. "The cloak was my thing to wrap around the chicks to protect them," he said. "The Doctor as mother hen."

Inevitably, it was the gradual evaporation of this family atmosphere that partly prompted his departure, which was announced in February 1974. Crucial to his decision were two things – the death in June 1973 of his good friend Roger Delgado, who played the Master, and the departure of Katy Manning, whose final episode was broadcast later the same week. These emotional leave-takings were echoed in the Third Doctor's moving death scene in *Planet of the Spiders*. "A tear, Sarah Jane?" he stammers. "No don't cry. Where there's life there's..."

"There are some idiots who seem to have problems with my time as the Doctor," he reflected in 1995. "In this business we call them casting directors." By that time, however, his own pet project, *Worzel Gummidge*, had long since proved a phenomenal hit and introduced him to a whole new generation of children. And in the meantime his allegiance to *Doctor Who* never really faded.

He demonstrated this in various ways – by appearing in the 1983 Special *The Five Doctors*, the 1989 stage show *Doctor Who: The Ultimate Adventure*, and two 1990s radio dramas, *The Paradise of Death* and *The Ghosts of N-Space*. He also became a flamboyant presence at conventions and was involved in the mooted 30th Anniversary Special *The Dark Dimension*, which to his horror devolved into a *Children in Need* item called *Dimensions in Time*. His disappointment was understandable; he was well aware of *Doctor Who*'s cultural impact, and more than once pointed out that the Doctor had become a genuine folkloric hero.

His sudden death, on 20 May 1996, came as a blow to the many fans who regarded Pertwee himself as a hero. Characteristically, his own estimate of the Third Doctor was more down to earth. "None of that Method crap" went into his performance, he observed. "However, I did believe in the Doctor. To maintain the magic you have to be able to believe it." ✳

Top: Pertwee protects some young competition winners from Aggedor during their visit to Television Centre in January 1972.

Above: The cover star of boys' comic *Countdown* in May 1971.

Right: "You put a Wor after W, and a Wor after O..." Pertwee in his favourite role, as hapless scarecrow Worzel Gummidge.

OTHER ROLES

THE NAVY LARK (1959-77)
This marathon radio comedy made Pertwee a household name, enshrining, among others, his classic comedy creations Weatherby Wett and Burbly Burwasher. Strangely, he wasn't featured in the 1959 film version.

CARRY ON SCREAMING! (1966)
One of four Carry Ons that Pertwee appeared in (the others being *Cleo*, *Cowboy* and *Columbus*), this features him in whiskery mode as a Scottish scientist who makes the fatal mistake of experimenting on Homo Gargantuosa.

THE HOUSE THAT DRIPPED BLOOD (1971)
Filmed between Pertwee's first and second seasons as the Doctor, the final segment of this four-story chiller cast him as an insufferably vainglorious horror star – a role originally earmarked for Vincent Price.

WHODUNNIT? (1974-78)
Pertwee presided over this Thames murder-mystery game show for five seasons. The title wasn't a punning nod to *Doctor Who*, incidentally; the original host, in 1973, had been Edward Woodward.

WORZEL GUMMIDGE (1979-81)
The Mummerset scarecrow was very much Pertwee's 'baby' and the series' huge success was a personal triumph. A two-season sequel, *Worzel Gummidge Down Under*, followed in 1987-89.

VIRTUAL MURDER: A TORCH FOR SILVERADO (1992)
Hungry for character roles, Pertwee lamented that "I'm having the devil's own job to persuade young directors that this is what I can do." His dying Spanish pyromaniac in this forgotten BBC series was a rare exception.

SCRIPTING THE THIRD DOCTOR

Early 1970s *Doctor Who* is not as formulaic as its detractors would suggest.

FEATURE BY **JUSTIN RICHARDS**

The *Dæmons* (1971) may be the most fondly remembered Third Doctor story, but it is by no means typical. The Third Doctor's time more than any other is coloured by the memory of just a few distinctive stories and elements. It's the UNIT era, featuring the classic ensemble line-up of the Doctor, Jo Grant, Brigadier Lethbridge-Stewart, Captain Yates and Sergeant Benton bravely battling, in a quintessentially English landscape, to scotch the Master's latest mad scheme. The Brigadier gets it all wrong and the Doctor saves the day with his sonic screwdriver by reversing the polarity of the neutron flow.

Except, of course, it isn't like that at all. Not usually.

The Dæmons is the only story set within the confines of an English village. The closest the Doctor gets to a similar setting is the rural Welsh

Opposite page: The Third Doctor stands between mankind and an alien race in *The Sea Devils* (1972).

Opposite page inset: "Give him a sign of your power, o mighty one." Miss Hawthorne (Damaris Hayman) and the Doctor in Episode Four of *The Dæmons* (1971).

Left: Oblivious to comments made by the Brigadier and Jo, the Doctor tries to fix the TARDIS dematerialisation circuit in Episode One of *Colony in Space* (1971).

Below left: The Doctor takes on Global Chemicals in *The Green Death* (1973).

Below: Jon Pertwee, Roger Delgado and an Axon, on location at Dungeness on 8 January 1971 for *The Claws of Axos*.

THE CONTINUING THREAD IS HIS BATTLE AGAINST BUREAUCRACY AND THE ESTABLISHMENT ITSELF.

community of *The Green Death* (1973). The UNIT 'family' as a whole are brought together for only seven of Jon Pertwee's 24 stories and after the first two seasons there are fewer stories with UNIT than without. If the Brigadier is occasionally wrong, it's for the right reasons. The sonic screwdriver is indeed a staple gadget, as is Bessie. But *The Sea Devils* (1972) is the only story of this era where the Doctor actually says he's reversed the polarity of the neutron flow.

The era can be divided, in the simplest terms, into the UNIT stories and the rest – the 'rest' usually being set in the future, though with occasional forays into the past. Where *The Dæmons* is perhaps more representative is in the collision of science and mythology, reason and magic. This is a theme explored in several stories including *The Curse of Peladon*, *The Time Monster* (both 1972) and *Planet of the Spiders* (1974).

But generally, the Third Doctor's earthbound stories are placed in a more industrial setting, facing a threat stemming from the misuse or misunderstanding of science. Stories like *Inferno* (1970) and *The Mind of Evil* (1971) reflect a contemporary scepticism about the speed of technological progress that the BBC series *Doomwatch* (1970-72) exploited with more depth and less humour. Even in stories where the threat is external – *Doctor Who and the Silurians*, *The*

Ambassadors of Death (both 1970), *The Claws of Axos* (1971), *The Time Monster* – a large part of the story takes place within a techno-scientific complex.

The stories set away from contemporary Earth are more diverse, but there is a thematic similarity that ties almost all the Third Doctor's adventures together. Perhaps incongruously for this most 'establishment' of Doctors, the continuing thread is his battle against bureaucracy and the establishment itself – whether it's the UNIT rules and regulations the Brigadier is bound by, the civil servants who wrap the Doctor in red tape, or the strictures of a future government or fading empire, as in *Frontier in Space* (1973) and *The Mutants* (1972). Big is bad – be it the aptly named Global Chemicals of *The Green Death* or the even wider Interplanetary Mining Corporation of *Colony in Space* (1971).

Although working within an organisation, the Doctor retains his individuality. Even without the backing of UNIT, he's central to every story – for the first time, the Doctor is happy to occupy the foreground and enjoy the limelight. No longer does he merely observe from the sidelines and intervene to correct the mistakes of others. Of course this leads to more extreme brushes with authority, landing him more often than not in trouble and behind bars.

For a Doctor who craves action and adventure, it's in these quieter moments when inaction is forced upon him that the Doctor tends to become philosophical and introspective. His stories of upsetting Henry VIII, of the day he found the "daisiest daisy" and came to realise the beauty of reality, anecdotes about being captured by the Medusoids, his tutorial to the Thal Codal on the nature of courage and bravery – these all come when the Doctor is imprisoned.

At a time where the programme's narrative was incident-driven, the Third Doctor is at his most Doctor-ish when the story pauses to catch its breath. ✳

DEATHWORLD

Before *The Three Doctors*, the original plans to celebrate *Doctor Who*'s tenth anniversary included a different story featuring William Hartnell, Patrick Troughton and Jon Pertwee...

FEATURE BY **ANDREW PIXLEY** ❧ ILLUSTRATION BY **MARK MADDOX**

"For years people had written in saying, Why don't you do a story with all three Doctors in?" recalled Terrance Dicks, script editor during the Jon Pertwee era of *Doctor Who*, when addressing devotees at the Who 1 Convention in Los Angeles in March 1980. "And I was saying, 'Nonsense' and chucking it on my reject pile.

"But there comes a time right at the beginning of every series when the script editor and producer sit down and make a very broad plan of what sort of stories they would like and who should write them. And [producer] Barry Letts and I came up with a few general ideas, and suddenly from out of the blue – I'd probably had too much wine for lunch or something – I said, 'What about this daft idea that the fans keep sending in about doing a show with three Doctors in? We couldn't really do that, could we?' And Barry said, 'No, we couldn't do that, it'd be too complicated... Well, maybe we could do it... Well, we could look into the *possibility* of doing it.' And the more we talked about it, the more of a good idea it seemed."

The fan-generated concept first came up soon after the arrival of Jon Pertwee's Doctor in January 1970. Being science fiction, *Doctor Who* was perhaps the only series in which a team-up between all the actors who had played the lead was really feasible. And it particularly appealed to Dicks and Letts because they always wanted a strong New Year gimmick to launch each fresh series of *Doctor Who*. For 1971 they'd created a new

arch enemy – the Master. Then they brought back the Daleks in 1972. And early that same year they were already thinking ahead to the show's tenth anniversary series for 1973.

Tentative approaches were made to Pertwee's predecessors, with Patrick Troughton indicating that he'd be delighted to resume the Second Doctor role and William Hartnell – now effectively retired through ill health – sounding similarly enthused about recreating the original Doctor. What the BBC production office didn't realise was that they'd caught the ailing Hartnell on one of his more lucid days.

"Terrance Dicks rang us up and asked us if we'd like to write a serial which involved all the Doctors," recalled Bob Baker in *The Doctor Who Review* in 1979. "We accepted it gladly. We'd watched Hartnell and Troughton, and I think we got a good line on them really."

Baker and his writing partner Dave Martin had already developed two *Doctor Who* serials for Dicks – both of which crammed an excess of ideas and concepts into large-scale narratives, prompting the BBC production office to remind the Bristol-based duo that "We're not MGM you know!" Now, the highly imaginative Baker and Martin had to come up with a way of getting the Third Doctor out of his UNIT laboratory in order to escape the earthbound exile imposed by the Time Lords.

On Thursday 3 February 1972 – shortly before their psychedelic new serial *The Mutants* started production – they ▶

Opposite page: The First, Second and Third Doctors face the horrors of *Deathworld*.

Below left: Producer Barry Letts, script editor Terrance Dicks and Jon Pertwee, on location at Peckforton Castle for *The Time Warrior* in May 1973.

Below: The Doctor (Jon Pertwee) and Jo Grant (Katy Manning) in Episode Four of *The Mutants* (1972).

DOCTOR WHO WAS PERHAPS THE ONLY SERIES WHERE A TEAM-UP BEWTEEN ALL THE ACTORS WHO HAD PLAYED THE LEAD WAS REALLY FEASIBLE.

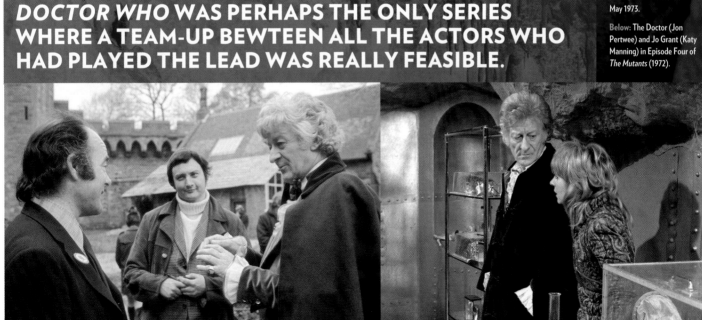

DEATHWORLD

BAKER AND MARTIN NOTED THAT THE INTERACTION BETWEEN THE DOCTORS COULD PROVIDE COMIC ELEMENTS TO COUNTERACT THE BATTLE AGAINST THE FORCES OF EVIL.

Above: Writers Bob Baker and Dave Martin proposed that the banter between the Doctors could provide some light relief in *Deathworld*. This idea was preserved with Patrick Troughton and Jon Pertwee in *The Three Doctors*.

Below: William Hartnell's ill health led to the restructuring of Baker and Martin's story, but Hartnell was able to join Troughton and Pertwee for this publicity shot on 9 November 1972.

submitted their 'three Doctors' proposal (headed *Idea for Next Season's Opener*) with a covering note that read, "As you know we are not very good at storylines but here is an idea we had on our last trip... on the train that is." Then came the pitch: "Assuming the three Doctors, we thought it would be logical that the only place they could meet would be somewhere out of time. This 'somewhere-out-of-time' we have assumed to be a kind of Underworld, Hades, Realms of Dis, Purgatorio – ie, the Afterworld, the World of Death..."

As such, their proposed narrative was boldly entitled *Deathworld*. The pitch continued with an outline of Episode One, opening with a pronounced echo of Ingmar Bergman's classic 1957 film *The Seventh Seal*. "Starts ... with a Game of Chess: the cowled figure of Death with his chalkwhite face and skeletal hands is playing the High King – or President – of the Time Lords." The High King, however, is playing with what Baker and Martin pointedly referred to as "three White Kings". As the first of the White Kings is taken, Death's bony fingers close around the captured piece – and, in a scribbled footnote, the writers rationalised this deviation from a normal chess match, in which the King cannot be taken. "*In this game, Death takes the King – not sporting, but that's Death...*"

The King's capture "causes an accident in the Doctor's Lab." Following the mishap, there's no sign of the Doctor or Jo Grant, and it's assumed their bodies were vaporised in the accident. "In fact they find themselves in Limbo – an eerie, ethereal empty sort of place." By the end of this first instalment, Death has disposed of the two other White Kings – "Doctor Who-Hartnell and Doctor Who-Troughton" – and they too have arrived in Limbo. Meanwhile, "Doctor Who-Pertwee" and Jo have "already been menaced and scared by one of Death's manifestations of himself..."

The proposal then outlined five areas of story development. The first notion put forward was that the Doctors have been allowed to enter the Underworld as a glorified initiative test; they're guinea-pigs in a struggle for power represented on one side by the Time Lords and on the other by the 'Forces of Evil' – a federation including Death, War, the Seven Sins, and various devils and Fates such as the Gorgon – who are plotting to overthrow the dominance of the Time Lords. The Time Lords believe that the gambling of one (or rather three) of their own kind is better than facing "an all-out interstellar war and

its consequent horrors for the ordinary, less-eternal people of the universe."

The second concept was that the Doctors don't know why they're in Limbo and that finding out is one of the tests they have to undergo. These challenges confront them with such figures as the Four Horsemen of the Apocalypse, zombies, demons and hobgoblins, all of whom, the Doctors realise, are manifestations of Death.

The third point, the writers went on, was that the escape from the Underworld is only accomplished through the combined efforts of all three incarnations. "Even so," they added, "Doctors Hartnell and Troughton sacrifice themselves so that the Doctor and Jo escape. Thus we have the two older Doctors appearing briefly in EPS ONE TWO AND THREE but figuring more largely in FOUR."

In the fourth strand, Baker and Martin noted that the interaction between the Doctors could provide comic elements to counterpoint the battle against the Forces of Evil. Furthermore, not all the manifestations of death need be terrifying. Drawing on Greek myths, they cited "the giant Polyphemus [which] could [be] rather blundering and stupid." In addition, the Seven Deadly Sins could also be used for comedic effect, just as they had been since medieval times, right up to the comedy sketch movie *The Magnificent Seven Deadly Sins*, released the previous year. ▶

BOB BAKER AND DAVE MARTIN

A former monumental mason turned house renovator and semi-pro saxophonist, Bob Baker formed a writing partnership with former hospital-worker turned advertising copywriter Dave Martin in 1967. After working on animated and live-action short films, their first television sale – to HTV in 1968 – was *Whistle For It*.

As well as contributing to the BBC comedy show *Whatever Next?*, they started writing regularly for *Doctor Who* after a commission in 1969, dreaming up such stories as *The Claws of Axos, The Mutants, The Sontaran Experiment, The Hand of Fear* and *The Armageddon Factor*. They also wrote episodes of ATV's *Hunter's Walk*, the BBC film series *Target* and such HTV titles as *Pretenders, Late Night Drama, Sky, King of the Castle, Follow Me* and *Murder at the Wedding*.

By mutual agreement, Baker and Martin split in 1978, shortly after creating the Doctor's robot dog, K-9, in *The Invisible Enemy*. Subsequently, Baker was script editor on the BBC's *Shoestring* and *Call Me Mister*, also working with HTV on *Into the Labyrinth, Jangles* and *Function Room*. In addition, he co-wrote several of Wallace and Gromit's award-winning animated adventures for Aardman Animation and co-created the 2009 non-BBC spin-off *K-9*.

Martin died in March 2007, while Baker published his autobiography, *K-9 Stole My Trousers*, in 2013.

Finally, the story as a whole would have elements in common with the 1969 serial *The War Games* through "the use of baddies from different zones and cultures". As such, the sinister mastermind of Death would manifest itself as mythological figures like the Hindu Goddess Kali and the Japanese spirit of the Spiderwoman.

"We put this idea up in this form – rather sketchy – at the moment to hear your reactions to the general concept of *Deathworld*," they concluded. "Our ideas on sets are still very vague: a sort of misty Limbo, the Caves of Hell, a kind of Haunted Castle … not much filming."

There was a lot here that Dicks liked – notably the brooding and enigmatic figure of evil that pervaded the story. But there was no way this figure could be Death, or indeed that such vivid depictions of evil and Limbo could be presented to a family audience within the show's budget and remit.

First, Death would become the figure of Ohm ('OHM' when rotated reads 'WHO', indicating the lead character's exact opposite), then Omega, the final entry in the Greek alphabet. The battle between an evil force and the all-powerful Time Lords was in. Limbo was out, replaced by a world of anti-matter. Certainly the first two Doctors couldn't sacrifice themselves, since in theory this would eliminate the possibility of the Third Doctor having ever existed. But certainly there could be an element of mystery as the different

THE BATTLE BETWEEN AN EVIL FORCE AND THE ALL-POWERFUL TIME LORDS WAS IN. LIMBO WAS OUT, REPLACED BY A WORLD OF ANTI-MATTER.

incarnations puzzle over a trap into which they're being drawn – albeit by the bad guy rather than their own race.

Another concern was the general tone. The writers were still cramming the various Forces of Evil into their Episode One draft script some three months later, prompting Dicks to explain to them that *Doctor Who* wasn't prepared to accommodate "mass suicides, corpse-filled morgues, lumbering ghastly zombies and man-eating fungus."

For want of a better name, *The Three Doctors* was adopted as a temporary working title for the four-part serial when it was commissioned by Dicks on Tuesday 27 June. Having read an article about the phenomenon of black holes in the 16 July edition of the *Sunday Times* ('Death Traps in Space' by Bryan Silcock), Baker and Martin established Omega's anti-matter world beyond the event horizon of such a super-dense mass, not even allowing light to escape its grip. This also gave the adventure a new title: *The Black Hole*.

Scheduled around the availability of Patrick Troughton, *The Black Hole* entered production in November 1972. By then, Dicks had been forced to amend Baker and Martin's script to reduce William Hartnell's involvement to just a few inserts that could be played back on monitors in studio – the final performance, as it turned out, of the 65-year-old actor's long career.

By the end of the month, when studio recording began, everyone had agreed that the celebratory venture needed a different title. A title that would make it clear that this serial encapsulated a whole decade of *Doctor Who*. A title that would proclaim its unique selling point loud and clear...

So, *The Three Doctors* it was then. ✵

Opposite page: The Second and Third Doctors confront Omega (Stephen Thorne) inside the black hole.

Opposite inset: "We will not attempt to leave this world before you do." The Second and Third Doctors strike a bargain with Omega to save the lives of the Brigadier (Nicholas Courtney), Mr Ollis (Laurie Webb), Dr Tyler (Rex Robinson), Jo Grant (Katy Manning) and Sergeant Benton (John Levene) in Episode Four of *The Three Doctors*.

Top: Hartnell, Troughton and Pertwee were first brought together for this *Radio Times* photo session, held at a studio in Battersea in October 1972.

Left: Stephen Thorne as Omega, the embittered Time Lord opponent of *The Three Doctors*.

HE HYPNOTISED HIMSELF
INTO BELIEVING THAT THE
DOCTOR AND TOM BAKER
WERE INDIVISIBLE.

TOM BAKER

Tom Baker imbued the Doctor with his own endearing eccentricity, taking the programme to new heights of popularity.

FEATURE BY **JONATHAN RIGBY**

Some actors get a bit neurotic when they are approached by people and called by the name of the character they play," mused Tom Baker in March 1978. "I don't mind being called Doctor Who – which I am all the time. I can't tell you just how dull life was when I was just Tom Baker."

He was talking to *Sunday Express* columnist Peter Dacre at the time, yet it was to Noel Edmonds, presenter of the BBC's *Multi-Coloured Swap Shop*, that he'd made an even starker admission some 18 months earlier. "I didn't discover myself," he sagely intoned, "until I got the part of Doctor Who."

In this he was echoing his immediate predecessor in the TARDIS, Jon Pertwee. Yet for Baker this identification with his signature role went extraordinarily deep.

The part became his on Pertwee's resignation in February 1974, and the process by which Baker merged identities with the Doctor began straight away. "I felt the best way to suggest I was an alien – and had dark thoughts, wonderful thoughts – was to be Tom Baker," he explained 25 years later. "And so that's what I did. And lots of people liked it, to my surprise."

This was an understatement. Given the combination of his own personal magnetism and an unrivalled seven-year commitment to the programme, he hypnotised not just himself into believing that the Doctor and Tom Baker were indivisible. He hypnotised the entire nation. So much so that, by 1978, he was able to tell Dacre that "I do not have an existence as Tom Baker."

Though Baker's existence seems to be a moot point even to the man himself, we can safely pin down its beginning to Saturday 20 January 1934, when Thomas Stewart Baker made his first appearance in Liverpool. Influenced by his Catholic mother, he soon graduated from incense-wreathed altar boy to trainee monk, only abandoning his dedication to the De La Mennais order, six years later, when he hit 21.

After National Service and a brief spot of drama training, he finally made his stage début, aged 32, in Edinburgh, playing the bear, among other roles, in *The Winter's Tale*. Not long afterwards he joined Laurence Olivier's National Theatre Company, making a hit as Don Quixote's horse in *The Travails of Sancho Panza*. "Things began to look up after that," he reflected later. "They let me play human beings."

Chief among these was the Prince of Morocco in the NT's 1970 production of *The Merchant of Venice*, which began the run of swarthy exotics for which Baker would be best known prior to being cast in *Doctor Who*.

First, Olivier recommended him for the showy role of Rasputin in the 1971 epic *Nicholas and Alexandra*, which, having been filmed in Spain, took Baker on a promotional tour of the USA. ("I was asked: 'How does a working-class boy like you adjust to an air-conditioned Cadillac?' I replied: 'Terribly easily.'") Then he ▶

Above: Tom Baker presents a 1979 episode of the Yorkshire Television series *The Book Tower*.

Opposite page: The Fourth Doctor (Tom Baker) faces the insidious Wirrn in *The Ark in Space* (1975).

Below left: Baker is collared by an old foe during his first photocall for *Doctor Who*, in February 1974.

Below: With Elisabeth Sladen (as Sarah Jane Smith) in a publicity shot from *The Seeds of Doom* (1976).

"I MAY ONLY BE A MIDDLE-AGED TEN-YEAR-OLD, BUT I TAKE *DOCTOR WHO* VERY SERIOUSLY."

Top: Hard times – the hod-carrying Baker and his gang of fellow builders, pictured in London in early February 1974.

Top right: The Doctor tinkers with part of the radio probe system in Part One of *Terror of the Zygons* (1975).

Above: As Long John Silver in the Mermaid Theatre's 1981 production of *Treasure Island*.

Right: Baker pays a visit to a young competition winner in March 1977.

played the Egyptian doctor in Bernard Shaw's *The Millionairess* (opposite Maggie Smith in the title role), which was the BBC's *Play of the Month* for September 1972.

By the time *The Millionairess* went out, Baker had filmed his scenes as the wicked magician Koura in *The Golden Voyage of Sinbad*, a rip-roaring mythological adventure that would eventually bring him to the attention of the BBC's Head of Drama Serials, Bill Slater. "When they offered me *Doctor Who*," Baker recalled, "I said 'Yes' like a shot. I was [working] on a building site at the time and handed in my hod with alacrity."

Despite high-profile roles like Rasputin and Koura, Baker's finances had dwindled. Indeed, he delightedly regaled journalists with details of his £6-a-week bedsit in Pimlico, together with the fact that, when starting out as the Doctor, "I was given a present. A girl in the BBC Wardrobe Department got me a white boiler suit to wear at rehearsals. She said it was smarter than the clothes I wear normally."

Making his début on 28 December 1974 in the first instalment of *Robot*, Baker's Doctor was an instant hit. A few adjustments had to be made, however, before he could really get into his stride. "The writers couldn't help themselves," he explained. "They were still writing for Jon. So naturally I had a certain influence about wrenching things my way or rephrasing them, and gradually they began to write towards me."

Here was a Doctor – mercurial, unpredictable, above all convincingly 'other' – who burned himself instantly into the minds of the many millions who saw him. The eccentric accoutrements – "my silly long scarf and my thyroid eyes" – were just that; much more important was the actorly zeal with which he fleshed out this fourth incarnation of the Doctor. "I may only be a middle-aged ten-year-old," he maintained, "but I take *Doctor Who* very seriously."

The middle-aged ten-year-old was plain to see, with the Doctor's fondness for jelly babies becoming almost as iconic as his voluminous scarf. ("There's actually something gruesome

Above: With new companion (and future wife) Lalla Ward, publicising *Destiny of the Daleks* in 1979.

Below: Promoting BBC2's *Doctor Who Night* in November 1999.

Below right: As Sherlock Holmes for ex-*Doctor Who* producer Barry Letts in *The Hound of the Baskervilles* (1982).

about eating something in the shape of a baby, but never mind.") But there was also a deeply serious, even sombre, side to Baker's Doctor, never better demonstrated than in his agonising moral dilemma at the end of the 1975 serial *Genesis of the Daleks*, when he can't bring himself to destroy the Kaled mutation room and thus stifle the Daleks at birth. "The real reason why I didn't kill the Daleks," Baker joked in 1999, "was that I would have destroyed Terry Nation's livelihood."

With his total absorption in the role, it was perhaps inevitable that Baker became increasingly 'difficult' in his later seasons. "It was simply that I got so proprietorial it was almost impossible to direct me," he admitted. And life imitated art in a very particular way when, on 13 December 1980, he married Lalla Ward, who played the Doctor's current assistant Romana. As it turned out, the marriage didn't long outlast Baker's tenure as the Doctor; having stepped down in March 1981, he split up with Ward 12 months later.

"Of course," Baker has observed ruefully, "I spent so much time reacting to monsters that when it came to going back to theatre and playing more ordinary people, I wasn't much good at it." This isn't quite true. In Baker's initial post-*Who* phase there was a lengthy tour for the Royal Shakespeare Company in *Educating Rita*, a return to the National Theatre in *She Stoops to Conquer*, and a double role as Sherlock Holmes and his arch-nemesis in *The Mask of Moriarty* in Dublin. And that was just the beginning.

Now, over 30 years after he relinquished the Doctor role, the question of Tom Baker's real existence is perhaps neither here nor there; vividly oracular, he's long since become a kind of national monument, capable of reducing any audience to hilarity within seconds. But there's no denying it – there's still an admixture of the Doctor in there, recalling the unique fusion of actor and role that took place between 1974 and 1981.

In its classic period, the leading part in *Doctor Who* passed from William Hartnell, a man keen to find a new identity as an actor, to Patrick Troughton, who, on the contrary, "didn't want anyone to know 'who' is playing Who." Next it was handed on to Jon Pertwee, one of whose autobiographies was categorically entitled *I Am the Doctor*, and then to an actor who would call his own memoirs *Who On Earth is Tom Baker?*

The profound effect the role had on these actors is testimony, perhaps, to the transformative power of that teasing *Who* in the programme's title. And of all the actors transformed by *Doctor Who*'s original run, Tom Baker remains arguably the most memorable and almost certainly the most popular. ✳

OTHER ROLES

NICHOLAS AND ALEXANDRA (1971)
Surrounded by some of Britain's best actors, Baker glowered impressively as the conniving quasi-holy man Rasputin in Franklin J Schaffner's sprawling account of the end of the Romanovs.

THE CANTERBURY TALES (1972)
The future Time Lord capered naked through this bawdy Chaucerian bacchanal for no less a director than Pier Paolo Pasolini. One of several Italian films Baker made around this time.

THE GOLDEN VOYAGE OF SINBAD (1973)
Following Patrick Troughton's example, Baker was here surrounded by Ray Harryhausen's extraordinary stop-motion marvels. Baker's showy role as a black-hearted magician had originally been mooted for Christopher Lee.

LATE NIGHT STORY (1978)
For Christmas week on BBC2, Baker was at his most sepulchral as the talking-head narrator of five creepy stories by Saki, Nigel Kneale, Ray Bradbury, Mary Danby and Graham Greene.

THE HOUND OF THE BASKERVILLES (1982)
Preceded by Peter Cushing and followed by Jeremy Brett in the annals of TV Sherlocks, Baker's Holmes was ill-served by this BBC version of *The Hound* – but it was an intriguing development from his Holmes-like Doctor in *The Talons of Weng-Chiang*.

MEDICS (1992-95)
Baker's role as Professor Hoyt in Granada's hospital drama was his first long-running TV commitment since *Doctor Who*, setting him up for such 21st-century engagements as *Strange*, *Little Britain* and *Monarch of the Glen*.

SCRIPTING THE FOURTH DOCTOR

This Doctor was a freewheeling renegade, in adventures that took the programme to the extremes of light and dark.

FEATURE BY **JUSTIN RICHARDS**

Where the Third Doctor was as often as not a 'front man' for an organisation, the Fourth Doctor is more of a loner, restricting himself for the most part to one or two companions. It makes narrative sense therefore that he generally faces not armies of monsters but a single villain, or 'spokesman' for the villains.

In *Genesis of the Daleks* (1975), for example, the Fourth Doctor is pitted not so much against the Daleks as against their creator Davros. *The Robots of Death* (1977) are led by a human, and by the 'co-ordinator' robot SV7, while the Egyptian 'Mummy' robots of *Pyramids of Mars* (1975) answer to Sutekh. In fact, the only monsters the Fourth Doctor meets who don't have a recognisable leader are the less than impressive Mandrels in *Nightmare of Eden* (1979) and the Marshmen of *Full Circle* (1980).

Opposite page: The typically enigmatic Fourth Doctor makes a surprise return to Gallifrey in *The Invasion of Time* (1978).

Opposite page inset: At the mercy of Sutekh (Gabriel Woolf) in Part Four of *Pyramids of Mars* (1975)

Left: The Doctor listens as Davros (Michael Wisher) contemplates ultimate power in Part Five of *Genesis of the Daleks* (1975).

Below left: Julian Glover as the ruthless Captain Tancredi, *aka* Scaroth, in *City of Death* (1979).

Below: "We're not going to turn you into scrap yet, are we Romana?" The Doctor, Professor Rumford (Beatrix Lehmann), Romana (Mary Tamm) attend to the stricken K9 in Part Two of *The Stones of Blood* (1978).

LUCKILY, THE FOURTH DOCTOR'S ERA ATTRACTED THESPIAN OPPONENTS OF THE HIGHEST CALIBRE.

There are good logistical reasons for this. It's obviously cheaper to create one alien enemy than a horde of them. And dramatically, it means that the Doctor can come into direct conflict, verbally as well as physically, with a single tangible threat. This in turn places a greater dependence on the writing of the villain, and the actor's performance; luckily, the Fourth Doctor's era attracted thespian opponents of the highest calibre.

Because it lasted so long, Tom Baker's tenure as the Doctor is more diverse than any other, with two distinct phases dictated by different production teams. Generally, the stories produced by Philip Hinchcliffe tend to be darker, while his successor Graham Williams introduced a lighter touch, bringing in wit and humour rather than horror.

To continue with generalisations, the earlier stories see the Doctor caught up in events – the Wirrn are already on board *The Ark in Space* (1975), the first Dalek is ready for action in *Genesis of the Daleks*, the Zygons have gone on the offensive in *Terror of the Zygons* (1975) and the Kraals seem to have invaded Earth in *The Android Invasion* (1975). Often the Doctor is less than happy to be involved; in *The Brain of Morbius* (1976), for example, he complains loudly that the Time Lords have dropped

him in it. But once persuaded of the threat he doesn't shirk.

Another recurring theme of this era is possession. Noah, turning into a Wirrn, gives the inarticulate creatures voice, just as Hieronymous becomes the mouthpiece for the Mandragora Helix in *The Masque of Mandragora* (1976). Friends becoming foes is an effective dramatic device, be it a duplicate Harry in *Terror of the Zygons* and *The Android Invasion* or Sarah possessed by Eldrad in *The Hand of Fear* (1976).

From *Horror of Fang Rock* (1977), when Williams took over as producer, the threat is generally less insidious. (The transition took a while, however, as Hinchcliffe's script editor Robert Holmes was still on hand initially – *Horror of Fang Rock*, *The Invisible Enemy* and *Image of the Fendahl* (all 1977) depict one or more 'possessed' characters.) In addition, the Doctor becomes more obviously proactive, happy to announce "I'm the Doctor" and hand round jelly babies rather than apparently sulking and wishing he was somewhere else.

The most obvious evidence of this change of emphasis is K9. Darker stories like *Genesis of the Daleks* or *The Talons of Weng-Chiang* have no place for a literal-minded robot dog. Similarly, K9 is off duty for the eerily atmospheric *Image of the Fendahl* and fits uneasily into *The Stones of Blood* (1978).

K9 is there to reassure younger viewers and to provide a sounding board for the Doctor, often defusing what tension remains as well as offering a ready escape from danger. As the production team changed again for the Fourth Doctor's final series, and new producer John Nathan-Turner determined to restore a more serious note to the programme, it's no coincidence that K9 was the first of many things he got rid of.

With such a wide variety of stories throughout the latter 1970s, it's the Fourth Doctor himself who gives continuity to the era via his recognisable silhouette, his wit and brilliance, and his unerring sense of justice. ✲

IN SEARCH OF
THE DOCTOR

The Doctor has been defined and redefined by successive production teams since 1963. One of the show's former script editors looks at how the character has changed.

FEATURE BY **ANDREW CARTMEL**

Doctor Who is the longest-running science-fiction series in television history. At its heart is its mercurial protagonist the Doctor, a unique blend of mischief-maker, explorer and action hero. He has been appearing on our screens for 50 years, yet he remains an enigma and a mystery.

We don't know his name, his true nature, or even – I would argue – where he comes from.

No mean feat, after half a century and countless adventures. He's at the centre of the show, yet he remains resolutely in shadow. So what can we say about this elusive character? Where does our search for him even begin?

Well, we know the Doctor through the stories that have been told about his exploits, so if we want to learn about him then our starting point must be with the people who shaped those stories.

Throughout the original run of Doctor Who the people most responsible for creating and

exploring the character of the Doctor were the programme's script editors.

Donald Tosh, now 78, was a story editor (as script editors were then called, not inaccurately) for the Doctor's first incarnation, William Hartnell. He began work during the second season of the show in 1965, following the series' highly influential first story editor, David Whitaker, and his successor Dennis Spooner. Tosh's run started with a crucial story, The Time Meddler.

It was a genuine thrill to talk to this man who did the same job as me all those years ago, back when *Doctor Who* was relatively new.

"He has to be an enigma and a mystery," says Tosh of the Doctor. This is a view I heartily endorse and which was to crop up again and again during this investigation. "But in a sense, by the time I took over on the show, Bill Hartnell had already developed this slightly crotchety, very clever but vague character. We had to remember that he was not just a maverick and a breakaway but also an incompetent, so we tried to add that into Bill Hartnell's actual portrayal. It meant, however clever he was, he would make basic mistakes like not understanding human beings, which would give us story possibilities.

"Later the Doctor became a much greater, god-like figure. But we deliberately didn't develop him

in that image. Our Doctor was always walking into trouble through his own incompetence. This was partly willed upon us in a sense by Bill himself, because by the time we took over he was feeling very insecure. His producer Verity Lambert had left and he was having trouble learning lines, and 'um-ed' and 'ah-ed' in his dialogue and so on.

"I remember discussing the character of the Doctor with David Whitaker. I spoke to him quite extensively before I took over. What I was doing was not letting Bill get too dominant, so that the Doctor would *become* Bill and thus be narrower. And also so the show could go on without him if necessary."

As well as conceiving an idea similar to regeneration, with all its far-reaching consequences, Tosh oversaw a story (his first) that would have a similarly profound effect. Dennis Spooner's *The Time Meddler* featured an adversary who was, for the first time, the Doctor's equal. He came from the same planet as the Doctor (although it was not yet called Gallifrey), he was also a maverick, he also had a TARDIS, and he

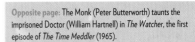

was also a Time Lord – although the term itself wouldn't appear for a few more years.

This was a big step because it meant the Doctor had gone from being a complete enigma to someone with a background, with a history he shared with others. Was Tosh aware what a major step this was? ▶

> ## "OUR DOCTOR WAS ALWAYS WALKING INTO TROUBLE THROUGH HIS OWN INCOMPETENCE."
> DONALD TOSH

REGENERATIONS

One of the things that makes *Doctor Who* unique, and which has allowed it to continue for 50 years, is the concept of regeneration. The Doctor can shed his old skin and emerge in a different form, to be played by a new actor with a new persona.

This all began with Donald Tosh and the necessity to deal with an ailing leading man. "I was

the first one to experiment with ideas of how to get Bill Hartnell out," he says. "We saw that Bill's health wasn't the best, but the show could go on without him. It didn't have to end if he left. And I strongly made the case that the transition – what would come to be called the regeneration – had to be seen on screen. I wrote a very long memo to my producer Johnny

Wiles about how to change the Doctor. You couldn't just have him walk out of the room and walk in as someone else. But you could use overlay effects to see him change. And then the kids would accept that."

Without Tosh's ingenuity the concept of regeneration might never have been developed, and *Doctor Who* might not be with us today.

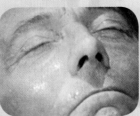

> ## "IF EVER THERE WAS A DOCTOR WHO MIGHT GO TO THE DARK SIDE IT WAS TOM."
> TERRANCE DICKS

"We were. That was very much Dennis Spooner and Verity Lambert's decision. Personally it's unlikely I would have done it. There were plenty of stories around, so we certainly didn't need to use the Doctor's background to come up with a plot this early in the series."

Was it a mistake to reduce the mystery of the Doctor?

"No," he says. "I think in fact we were wrong not to create more of a back-story than we did by the time we handed over to the next production team. They needed more of a structure to build the Doctor from. We should have gone a little down the route they did when they later created Gallifrey."

Next I spoke to a man who was there when the programme did indeed name the Time Lords and create Gallifrey – Terrance Dicks. Dicks became a script editor for Patrick Troughton's Doctor in late 1968, and remained in the post for the whole of Jon Pertwee's tenure. Like Donald Tosh, he would be involved in an absolutely pivotal *Doctor Who* story. In Dicks' case, *The War Games*.

At this point in the show's history, the meddling Monk with his TARDIS might have been a one-off, never to be repeated. But with *The War Games* the Time Lords, as they were now called, had arrived in force. And they were here to stay.

"The Doctor is always the same," Dicks maintains. "His character changes with each actor but only on the surface – the quirks. Underneath he is upright, decent, on the side of good. Never unkind, cruel or cowardly. In short, a hero."

Did he ever speculate about who this mysterious figure really was?

"I know who he was. A Time Lord from Gallifrey who fell out with his fellows because he couldn't stand their devious ways. And so he decided to forsake them and take off in the TARDIS. That's all he is. I'm very much against this tendency to turn him into an inexplicable, god-like, alien figure."

Did Patrick Troughton shape his thinking of the Doctor's character?

"The Doctor was always the Doctor. Once you know who is cast you almost unconsciously adapt to his style. Pat Troughton was more lovable than Hartnell and there was the danger that he'd be too kindly and avuncular. But Pat was too good an actor. He could avoid that. At a moment of drama he could be powerful or frightening.

"Pertwee was elegant and dandyish but occasionally you got a glimpse of steel with him too. When I first met Tom Baker I was very struck with his zany style, so I built that in. But if ever there was a Doctor who might go to the dark side it was Tom. The zaniness could modulate into madness. I don't think it ever did, but you had the feeling that it might. The Peter Davison Doctor could never go to the dark side. More than the others he had a quality of decency and

Opposite page above: The Third Doctor (Jon Pertwee) in *The Sea Devils* (1972).

Opposite page below: Omega takes the appearance of the Fifth Doctor (Peter Davison) in Part Four of *Arc of Infinity* (1983).

Above left: The Fourth Doctor (Tom Baker) with Co-ordinator Engin (Erik Chitty) and Castellan Spandrell (George Pravda) in Part Four of *The Deadly Assassin* (1976).

Above: The Seventh Doctor (Sylvester McCoy) in the shadows cast by *Ghost Light* (1989).

Below: Tenth Doctor David Tennant tries Time Lord robes on for size during a break in recording *The Sound of Drums* (2007).

Left: The Sixth Doctor (Colin Baker) challenges the Valeyard in *The Trial of a Time Lord* (1986).

uprightness, transparent honesty. An English gentleman really." He laughs. "We assume that God is an Englishman."

I always feel a combination of guilt and amusement when Dicks mentions the inexplicable, all-powerful, utterly mysterious Doctor and how much he dislikes that interpretation. Because it's an interpretation I was pretty much responsible for introducing. When I took over as script editor in 1986 the Doctor was in trouble. He was in danger of being overwhelmed by the Time Lords and his own convoluted history.

Indeed, just before I joined he'd been put in the dock by his fellow Gallifreyans in *The Trial of a Time Lord*. Seeing him like that was like seeing a tiger in a cage, but the tiger's teeth had been pulled. Through a series of accidents, mistakes and good ideas gone wrong, the Doctor seemed to me to have become a victim, a fall guy. He was in danger of becoming a clown – and not the beguiling Patrick Troughton style of clown.

So I made a point of simultaneously building the Doctor up and shrouding him in shadow. With Sylvester McCoy in the role, and through the work of the excellent writers I hired (Marc Platt, Ben Aaronovitch, Ian Briggs and others), I was able to make the Doctor powerful and enigmatic. In

our scripts we dropped hints that the Doctor's role as a Time Lord was just that – a pose, a disguise. He didn't really come from Gallifrey and was far more than a Time Lord. He was something dangerous, immense and unknown.

Following on from us, decades later, it was soon evident that Russell T Davies had drawn similar conclusions. Davies was *Doctor Who*'s showrunner from 2005 to 2010, providing the same creative guidance as the previous script editors. He understood that the Doctor had to stand alone and that the presence of the Time Lords as his equals – or, worse, his superiors – was a fatal threat to that. But he took an approach utterly unlike mine.

Rather than altering the Doctor's personal history to change our perspective on the Time Lords, he removed them from the picture altogether by wiping them out in the Time War. It was an entirely different method, but just as effective in giving the Doctor back his uniqueness.

And what of today's showrunner, Steven Moffat? How does he see the Doctor?

"I think the Doctor is a role that requires more inventiveness per day than any other part," he says. "You've got to play it sincerely, emotionally and truthfully, but you've also got to be an entertainer. You've got to find a mad thing to do every single day; if you come through a door you have to do it in a Doctor-ish way. You've got to find an interesting spin on what amounts to a page-and-a-half of exposition.

"The Doctor is a character who can always come back," he adds. "Goodness knows you're not wedded to a particular actor, you're not even wedded to a particular style.

"The show is like a beautifully robed predator that can dispose of anybody who works on it – none of us matters *a damn*. You give your all to *Doctor Who*, and the moment you leave it, it just carries on as if you'd never been there. Like any great predator it adapts to the landscape perfectly and instantly. In 50 years from now, if we're still around to see it – in which case I'll be phenomenally old – *Doctor Who* will be almost unrecognisable in some ways, but will fit perfectly into whatever television world exists at that point.

"That's why," Moffat concludes, "it will always be around." ✳

DAVISON IS SUPERB AS THE NEWLY TRANSFORMED DOCTOR – VULNERABLE, BEWILDERED, ONLY GRADUALLY SHOWING HIS METTLE.

PETER DAVISON

Peter Davison's relative youth made him a surprising choice for the Fifth Doctor, but he impressed fans and critics with a thoughtful and detailed portrayal.

FEATURE BY **DAVID MILLER**

If Patrick Troughton faced a daunting task in making the first change of lead actor in *Doctor Who*, then following Tom Baker as the Doctor must have been almost as nerve-wracking.

Baker's replacement was 29-year-old Peter Davison, a popular actor who had specialised in playing amiable young men, most notably Tristan Farnon in *All Creatures Great and Small*, the hit BBC series about a Yorkshire veterinary practice in the 1930s. *Doctor Who* producer John Nathan-Turner, who supervised Tom Baker's last season, had worked as a Production Unit Manager on *All Creatures* and knew Davison well. "Peter is so right for *Doctor Who*," he told the press. "He is very popular with children and has a large following with feminine viewers."

Davison had private doubts about his suitability, feeling he was too young, but Nathan-Turner impressed on him the need for contrast.

Davison's casting made the BBC News on 4 November 1980, following an announcement about another actor in a big part – Ronald Reagan, newly elected as the 40th president of the United States. Davison's fame in *All Creatures* was a gift to hard-pressed headline writers, and the next day *The Sun* gave us 'Dr Moo'. Later *Time Out* made a more intelligent comparison between Davison's Doctor and the Bonzo Dog Doo-Dah Band's eccentric front man Vivian Stanshall.

Scripting problems meant that Davison's post-regeneration story was made fourth in the schedule for his first series. This at least allowed the actor three stories to settle in and delineate the new Doctor's character. The plan worked. In his début adventure, *Castrovalva*, Davison is superb as the newly transformed Doctor – vulnerable, bewildered, only gradually showing his mettle. His impersonations of the previous Doctors are particularly charming.

Scriptwriter Christopher Bidmead's notion of "an old man in a young body" was underlined by the Doctor's occasional wearing of half-spectacles, and Heather Hartnell remarked that Davison seemed "like a younger version" of her late husband William.

Davison was the first of the actors cast as the Doctor to have watched the series as a child, and recalled Patrick Troughton's performance with great fondness. Davison professed to dislike the "instant miraculous solutions" that had been a feature of Baker's years and wanted to bring back an element of suspense. "My Doctor will be flawed," he said. "He will have the best intentions and will in the end win through, but he will not always act for the best. Sometimes he will even endanger his companions. But I want him to have a sort of reckless innocence." ▶

Above: At 29, Peter Davison was younger than any of his predecessors as the Doctor.

Opposite page: Peter Davison as the Fifth Doctor in *Castrovalva* (1982).

Below left: Nyssa (Sarah Sutton), Tegan (Janet Fielding), the Doctor and Adric (Matthew Waterhouse) in *Castrovalva*, the Fifth Doctor's first televised story.

Below right: The terrible fate of Plantagenet (Jeff Rawle) becomes clear in *Frontios* (1984).

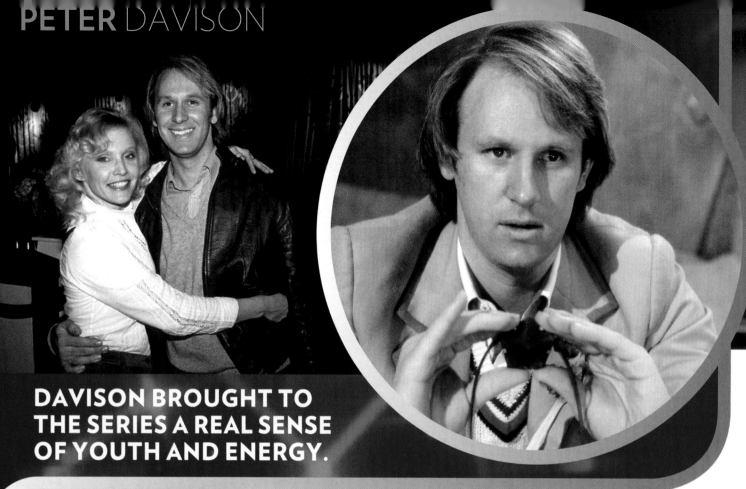

DAVISON BROUGHT TO THE SERIES A REAL SENSE OF YOUTH AND ENERGY.

Top: Davison with his first wife Sandra Dickinson. Photo © Rex/Sten Rosenlund.

Top right: The Doctor prepares to challenge the Mara in *Snakedance* (1983).

Right: Davison pictured outside the BBC's Acton rehearsal rooms on 28 July 1983, the day he announced his departure from *Doctor Who*.

Above: With Christopher Timothy and Robert Hardy in *All Creatures Great and Small*. Photo © Rex/John Sherbourne/Daily Mail.

Davison was born Peter Moffett in Streatham on 13 April 1951 and attended the Winston Churchill School in Woking. His father worked in electronics and the young Peter was interested in music and recording his own songs. He studied at the Central School of Speech and Drama, spent a year in repertory at the Nottingham Playhouse and then a season on tour with the Edinburgh Young Lyceum Company.

In April 1975 he made one of his earliest television appearances, in ITV's science-fiction series *The Tomorrow People*, wearing a pair of blue underpants and a bubble perm wig. Davison pointed out that he got the part by tagging along to the audition with his girlfriend Sandra Dickinson, who was cast as his sister Emily. The couple were married in 1978 and had a daughter, Georgia, in 1984.

Higher calibre television work quickly followed. There was a prominent role in a serialisation of HE Bates' *Love for Lydia* in 1977, then later that year he was cast in *All Creatures Great and Small*. He also appeared in two sitcoms, as a stay-at-home dad in LWT's *Holding the Fort* with Patricia Hodge, and as would-be intellectual Brian in *Sink or Swim* for the BBC. There was a point, Davison noted, when he was on television in a different programme almost every day of the week.

Then came *Doctor Who*, and his arrival wasn't the only change in the programme to cause ripples. To howls of protest, the series was moved from its traditional Saturday night slot to Mondays and Tuesdays. Davison's first season as the Doctor was a huge success, however, with several strong stories and

the return of the Cybermen helping to pacify even the most demanding fans.

Davison brought to the series a real sense of youth and energy after the doom-laden atmosphere of Tom Baker's last stories, and the ratings leapt. Soon, his face replaced Baker's on a cornucopia of posters, t-shirts, jigsaw puzzles and other *Who* merchandise. There was also the excitement of the series' upcoming 20th anniversary, which was celebrated with a special story featuring previous Doctors Patrick Troughton and Jon Pertwee.

The anniversary aside, Davison's second season, hit by strikes, low budgets and scripting problems, was a dispiriting time, and Davison decided that he would leave at the end of his third year. In doing so he was following the advice of Patrick Troughton, who said three years was enough if he wanted to resume his career with any success. An injection of cash from BBC Enterprises made that third year more spectacular, and the Fifth Doctor went out on a resounding high note

OTHER ROLES

ALL CREATURES GREAT AND SMALL
(1978-90)
Though Davison later admitted that he was absolutely no good with animals, by far his longest television role was as vet Tristan Farnon, well-meaning muddler and would-be Lothario of the Dales.

THE HITCH HIKER'S GUIDE TO THE GALAXY (1981)
With his wife Sandra Dickinson cast as Trillian in the TV version of Douglas Adams' SF comedy, Davison took a cameo as the Dish of the Day at the Restaurant at the End of the Universe. He played a doleful space cow who positively *wants* to be eaten.

A VERY PECULIAR PRACTICE (1986-88)
Davison played idealistic medic Stephen Daker in Andrew Davies' scathing satire of university life, heading a peerless cast including Graham Crowden, David Troughton and Barbara Flynn. One of the television benchmarks of the 1980s.

CAMPION (1989-90)
Margery Allingham's 1930s novels featuring gentleman detective Albert Campion made an elegant vehicle for Davison in 1989. Brian Glover was an excellent foil as Campion's safe-cracking manservant, with Michael Gough and Mary Morris among the guest stars.

THE LAST DETECTIVE
(2003-05)
Davison is often cast to good effect as disappointed – or disappointing – men, and was the perfect embodiment of Leslie Thomas' hapless Inspector 'Dangerous' Davis in *The Last Detective*. He inherited the role from Bernard Cribbins, who had previously played Davis in a one-off drama.

LAW & ORDER: UK (2011-13)
From the fifth series of *Law and Order UK*, the British spin-off of the long-running US crime series, Davison was cast as Henry Sharpe, the principled Director of the London Crown Prosecution Service. Davison brought humour and gravitas to the role and in his first episodes co-starred with a former *Doctor Who* companion, actress Freema Agyeman.

in his final adventure, *The Caves of Androzani*.

After *Doctor Who*, Davison was rarely short of work. He returned to *All Creatures Great and Small* for three more seasons, together with leading roles in *Anna of the Five Towns*, *A Very Peculiar Practice* and *Campion* that saw him into the 1990s. "I think the secret is that I've been able to move easily from one genre to another," he told an American interviewer. "A lot of actors get unfairly stuck in sitcoms, or very serious drama, or soap operas, and I've managed to dodge from one thing to another."

In 1999, Davison joined Colin Baker and Sylvester McCoy in *The Sirens of Time*, the first of an ongoing series of full-cast audio plays produced by Big Finish. The Fifth Doctor acted as the elder statesman to stop the squabbles between the 'junior' Doctors and Davison admitted that he was delighted to join in.

"The BBC had effectively dropped *Doctor Who* and this filled a very important gap in the market," he said. He has now recorded nearly 50 Big Finish adventures, and praises the high quality of the writing. "If I had a chance to go back and do my original *Doctor Who* stories I'd do them again. So this is a chance to make up for any shortcomings in the original stories that we did."

In 2007, in a specially recorded scene for *Children in Need* with Davison and David Tennant, the Fifth and Tenth incarnations of the Doctor met. It was a poignant encounter – Tennant was a longstanding fan of *Doctor Who* and Davison's Doctor in particular. The following year, Tennant met Davison's daughter Georgia, now an actress, when she appeared in the revived series; the couple were married in 2011.

As of 2013, Davison has married again and has two young sons. He is still busy, with a regular role as senior lawyer Henry Sharpe in *Law and Order UK*, more Big Finish productions and a worldwide roster of convention appearances for the show's 50th anniversary. But despite being one of the most prolific television actors of his generation, he is happy to be best remembered as the Fifth Doctor. ✳

Top: Davison considers that his final story, *The Caves of Androzani* (1984), was also his best.

Above: A signed publicity postcard, featuring an image from *The Visitation* (1982).

Right: As Dr Stephen Daker in *A Very Peculiar Practice* (1986-88).

SCRIPTING THE FIFTH DOCTOR

During the early 1980s *Doctor Who* was both experimental and steeped in nostalgia.

FEATURE BY **JUSTIN RICHARDS**

The Fifth Doctor's era continues the trend, begun in Season 18 (1980-81), towards more serious adventures. More than that, it's a period that values concept above story.

This is apparent right from the start. *Castrovalva* (1982) – like several other Fifth Doctor stories – is named after its setting. The starting point, for the first time in *Doctor Who*'s history, is not the narrative. As with other stories, including *Kinda*, *Time-Flight* (both 1982), *Snakedance*, *Mawdryn Undead* and *Enlightenment* (all 1983), the adventure is driven not by strictures of plot and character but by what is necessary to explore a concept or an environment.

This usually works well and the narrative picks up on and expands the thematic underpinnings. But sometimes a tension exists between maintaining the dramatic pace and exploring

THE MOST RESONANT STORIES TEND TO BE THE MORE ACTION-ORIENTATED, LESS CEREBRAL ADVENTURES.

the ideas. The distorted world of *Castrovalva* might reflect the fractured personality of Peter Davison's regenerating Doctor, but the first two episodes offer little more than runaround and red herring. The environment and clashing cultures of *Four to Doomsday* (1982) are fascinating in their own right, but the story that provides the excuse for their exploration is woefully thin.

Far more successful are Christopher Bailey's twin Mara stories – *Kinda* and *Snakedance* – which create a drama of their own while expanding on their respective themes and motifs. But in all these stories there are times where the Doctor is less than central to the plot and often irrelevant to the resolution.

So the most resonant stories from the Fifth Doctor's era tend to be the more action-oriented, less cerebral adventures, the ones that play to the series' traditional strengths, among them *The Visitation* (1982), *The Five Doctors* (1983), *Resurrection of the Daleks* (1984) and the story that defines the Fifth Doctor's time – *Earthshock* (1982).

Structurally, these are all very straightforward narratives. A threat is established and the Doctor gets involved (and probably locked up). There's a moment when it seems the villains have triumphed, usually at the end of the third instalment, as Omega assumes control of the

Matrix, or the Silurians take charge of the Seabase, or the Cybermen arrive in strength.

Then, in a thrilling final episode, the Doctor saves the day and defeats the enemy – more often than not in a fairly simplistic manner. The Terileptils are defeated in a fight and a fire, Omega is shot, the Daleks are defeated when the Movellan virus is released, the Silurians and Sea Devils succumb to handy Hexachromite gas...

Leaving aside the deliberately celebratory *The Five Doctors*, this was a period when the programme relied heavily on continuity and resurrecting foes – and friends – from the past. Despite this, there are no recurring villains within the Fifth Doctor's tenure apart from the Black Guardian, whose three appearances form a single narrative, and the Master, who pops up in five unconnected stories. Unlike the Third Doctor's time, the Master in this era tends not to side with alien baddies but takes control himself.

This is an era of contradictions. The 'high concept' stories sit side by side with action-adventure. Important plot points like the Master's reappearance or how a space freighter can travel back in time are glossed over while the main stories suffer from over-complication – *Resurrection of the Daleks* being a prime offender.

Old and new pull in different directions, so that when Season 20 (1983) proudly boasts a returning element in every story, the emphasis is actually on visuals and production gloss rather than narrative resonance.

But when these elements come together – the mixture of old and new, of driving narrative and underlying concept, the marriage of accomplished production with striking set-piece action – then the formula is unbeatable.

The Fifth Doctor may be backgrounded for the main narrative of his final story *The Caves of Androzani* (1984), but that detail becomes pivotal to his character. Never mind the fate of the tragic Sharaz Jek – the Doctor doesn't spare him a glance. This is a Doctor who will willingly lay down his life for his friend, and the rest of the adventure can go on around him as he moves Heaven and Androzani Minor to that end. ✳

THE SIX DOCTORS

The 20th anniversary of *Doctor Who* was originally due to be celebrated with a story by the doyen of the show's scriptwriters, Robert Holmes.

FEATURE BY **ANDREW PIXLEY** ● ILLUSTRATION BY **MARK MADDOX**

Opposite page: Doctors Two, Three, Four and Five discover that their predecessor is a robot imposter in *The Six Doctors*.

Below: The Master (Anthony Ainley) in the 1983 story *The King's Demons*.

Bottom left: Tegan (Janet Fielding), the 2nd Mutant (Brian Darnley) and the Fifth Doctor (Peter Davison) in the final episode of *Mawdryn Undead* (1983).

Bottom right: The Cyber Leader (David Banks) and Cyber Lieutenant (Mark Hardy) plan their attack in Part Two of *Earthshock* (1982).

By July 1982, *Doctor Who* script editor Eric Saward, having viewed earlier archival adventures in space and time, was beginning to admire one writer in particular.

"I became aware of how good Robert Holmes' stuff was," he commented several years later. "Now just before this happened, [producer] John [Nathan-Turner] had got the go-ahead to do the 90-minute 20th anniversary thing, and I suggested we approach Robert Holmes. Robert had worked with [Patrick] Troughton, [Jon] Pertwee, Tom Baker... knew them and written for them. Bob to me seemed an absolutely splendid choice."

Normally reluctant to use writers pre-dating his period at the helm, Nathan-Turner agreed that a knowledge of the show's history was essential for this particular assignment, so Holmes – himself a former *Doctor Who* script editor – was invited to come in for a story discussion.

In late July, Nathan-Turner began booking actors for the special, including the regular cast of Fifth Doctor Peter Davison and Janet Fielding, who portrayed the Doctor's companion Tegan. Also signed up were Third Doctor Jon Pertwee and Anthony Ainley, who was then appearing on a semi-regular basis as the Doctor's arch enemy, the Master.

The title ascribed to the project at this time was *The Six Doctors*, stirring speculation about a potentially new incarnation of the Time Lord but in fact referring to a fake version of the First Doctor over and above the five 'true' Doctors. Since William Hartnell had died in April 1975, the real First Doctor would be seen in footage from existing episodes, with a new actor cast as a robot lookalike.

Aware that references to the show's long history were popular with the dedicated fan base, Nathan-Turner's plan was not only to feature one fake and five real Doctors, but also numerous companions – notably Susan (the original Doctor's granddaughter, played by Carole Ann Ford) and Jamie (the Second Doctor's loyal sidekick, portrayed by Frazer Hines). Ranked against the forces of good, he envisaged an alliance between the Master and the Cybermen, the cyborg menace that had been warmly received when reintroduced in *Earthshock* just a few months earlier. ▶

THE REAL FIRST DOCTOR WOULD BE SEEN IN FOOTAGE FROM EXISTING EPISODES, WITH A NEW ACTOR CAST AS A ROBOT LOOKALIKE.

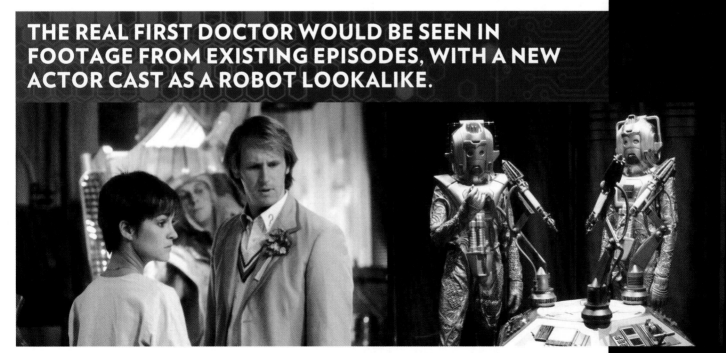

Above: Sarah Jane Smith (Elisabeth Sladen) in the 20th Anniversary Special *The Five Doctors* (1983).

Right: The Master (Anthony Ainley) turns the tables on the Cyber Leader (David Banks) in *The Five Doctors*.

Below: Robert Holmes, pictured in 1974.

Bottom left: An Auton, one of Holmes' creations from his 1970 story *Spearhead from Space*.

Bottom right: Mr Sin (Deep Roy) from Holmes' 1977 classic *The Talons of Weng-Chiang*.

"I remember when Bob walked into the office," Saward recalled in 1988. "He came in – a big man, tall, ex-policeman many years ago – and he still had that presence. I think he looked at John and I and thought, Crikey, a couple of real jerks here!"

A believer in new ideas, Holmes didn't like recycling elements of the show's past and was particularly concerned by the 'Master plus Cybermen' concept. According to Saward, Holmes (no doubt recalling his unhappy rewrites on *Revenge of the Cybermen* in 1974) exclaimed, "Forget it, the Cybermen are stupid, they don't work very well and I like creating original characters."

The meeting was an awkward one. Holmes was keen to work on *Doctor Who* again but was less than convinced about the practicality of including so many characters in a coherent plotline. "The brief was lunatic," Saward later admitted, "and of course Bob Holmes just fell on the floor laughing because it was so bloody stupid."

Nevertheless, on Monday 2 August Holmes was commissioned to develop a scene breakdown for '*The Six Doctors* (working title) – A 90-minute special programme celebrating *Doctor Who*'s 20th Year', to be delivered three weeks later. Unfortunately, he was still fundamentally unhappy with the brief and was unable to come up with a storyline, telephoning Saward on Tuesday the 24th to apologise for non-delivery. Saward suggested that if he could submit something by the following Tuesday, they could convene for a discussion the next day, Wednesday 1 September.

"The main problem we face," began Holmes' untitled proposal, "is to find a satisfactory and plausible explanation for all the Doctors, plus companions, appearing at the same point in the space-time continuum. I feel that this – dramatically – is what our audience will expect. However, the clash of mighty egos [of the actors involved] has been mentioned and

HOLMES DIDN'T LIKE RECYCLING ELEMENTS OF THE SHOW'S PAST AND WAS PARTICULARLY CONCERNED BY THE 'MASTER PLUS CYBERMAN' CONCEPT.

ROBERT HOLMES

Finlay's Casebook prior to becoming a regular writer on *Doctor Who* from 1968.

Having written highly acclaimed stories like *Spearhead from Space* and *The Time Warrior*, he joined the programme as script editor from 1973 to 1977, during which time he wrote such favourites as *The Ark in Space* and *The Talons of Weng-Chiang*. As well as script editing *Armchair Thriller* and *Shoestring*, he wrote for, among others, *Public Eye* and *Blake's 7*, continuing to contribute serials to *Doctor Who* up to his death in 1986.

Born in Hertfordshire in 1926, Robert Holmes served in the Queen's Own Cameron Highlanders, then joined the police force after the war before moving into journalism and working on *John Bull* magazine. Around 1960 he started writing for television, working on series such as *Knight Errant '60*, *The Saint* and *Doctor*

it is possible for them to appear in the same story without appearing together. The purpose of this discussion document is to survey the various options open to us."

Holmes' first option opened with the First Doctor on the planet Maladoom ("Doctor Will and companion striding across a misty landscape"). While the Doctor is busy "pointing out various botanical features and making deductions about the nature of the planet," it's revealed that all this is just an image on a screen, with "voices of unseen watchers" commenting admiringly ("Really remarkably lifelike"). Thus was explained the absence of the original actor to have played the Doctor. "Eventually, about an hour from now," noted Holmes, "we shall learn that Doctor Will and Carol Ann [sic] are cyborgs, created by cyber-technology. This will explain why the Doctor is not quite as we remember Hartnell."

Meanwhile, back with the current Doctor... The Time Lord is helpless at the controls of his TARDIS while explaining to Tegan that the vessel is being drawn into a time vortex that could mean destruction. "Maybe we do some clever mirror-work and show more than one police box whirling down this sudden fissure in the ordered universe," suggested Holmes. The TARDIS arrives on Maladoom with the Doctor furious about the "irresponsible idiot [who has been] interfering with the delicately balanced polarity of time and matter." Knowing that this dangerous lunacy "could create chaos," the Doctor determines to put a stop to it.

In due course, the other three Doctors arrive with their companions, and the fourth incarnation – "Doctor Tom" – speculates that another race has discovered "the power previously known only to Time Lords." United, they set off to put a halt to it. Meanwhile, the Fifth Doctor and Tegan head across rough terrain in the direction of a light pulsing from inside a craggy hillside. They discover "a rectangular panel of some shiny black substance" set into the rockface, and as they examine it they're rendered unconscious by concealed vapour jets when the panel opens. The remaining Doctors are then captured in similar automated traps.

With the Doctors and their companions lying unconscious in a cryogenic chamber, the Master gloats over the fact that "all the time entities that comprise the total Doctor" are at his mercy. Just by turning the freezer down he could finish off his oldest adversary for good, only he doesn't dare because of his current pact with the Cybermen.

The Second Doctor – "Doctor Pat" – is taken to an operating theatre where the Cybermen prepare him for surgery with a reviving injection. The Cybermen make preliminary tests to find the organic mechanism that separates Time Lords from other species. When they find it they will separate it and implant it into their familiar cybernetic machinery, thus turning themselves into Cyberlords."

At this point the Second Doctor goes into "terminal collapse" and is pronounced dead. The Cybermen are unconcerned; they expected to lose a few Doctors before isolating "the vital organ", hence their recruitment of the Master to capture all the Doctors from their "various time loops."

As it transpires, the Second Doctor has entered a "self-willed cataleptic state" and recovers when returned to the cryogenic chamber. There he disconnects the freezer panels to revive his fellow captives, who realise that they're trapped in the Master's temporal paradox. Having reconsidered the medical procedure, the Cybermen arrive to collect the Third Doctor –

"Doctor Jon" – but are overpowered by the revived prisoners.

The next part of the narrative, planned to be shot on film, consists of a "trial by ordeal" in which the Cybermen hunt the Doctors, all of whom are making for the shining hill to restore the time-space continuum before permanent damage is done to the universe. When the fake cyborg – "Doctor Will" – attempts to lead the group into an ambush, he's exposed as an impostor and falls off a cliff ("his springs fall out"). Susan is similarly exposed, to the disappointment of Jamie ("Frazer"), who was getting to rather like her.

The strange hill, once reached, is revealed to be a mass of technology linked to the Master's TARDIS, massively increasing its power and creating the time vacuum which captured the Doctors. However, it's now feeding on itself ("like a nuclear reactor running out of control") and likely to implode into a black hole.

"We've all been through this one before," Holmes commented. "The Master will, of course, turn up to provide some last-moment impediment. But, in the end, the Doctors get the machinery into phase before it goes critical. As it slows they, together with their appropriate companions, disappear back into their own sectors of time – the relative dimensions effect." This leaves the Fifth Doctor and Tegan alone at the end of the adventure.

"The sharp-eyed reader will ask what happened to the Cybermen," added Holmes. "Well, we won't have that many to start with. Some will be blown up when the Doctors escape because, before departing, they sabotage the operating theatre. Others will be disposed of variously – buried under rock-falls, sunk in swamps, pushed off cliffs and so on – during the film chase."

Holmes' second option was the same general story, "but we open with the present Doctor and stay with him until the operating theatre scene." Then, when the Cybermen tamper with the Doctor's metabolism, he regresses through his various "phases" ("first into Doctor Tom, then into Doctor Jon and so on") as he escapes, fights the Cybermen and makes for the shining hill. "When he reaches his Doctor Will incarnation he knows he is on his last legs. If he doesn't make it before his time runs out, he will finally be dead. (This, too, offers a possible explanation as to why he doesn't exactly resemble the real Hartnell.)"

This story, Holmes maintained, was attractive because it meant that the Doctors would never have to meet up. He admitted, however, that it would be difficult having Tegan turn into earlier companions. "Maybe mental projection? In each of his forms he would see the companion he had at that time."

The third – and shortest – option involved using the TARDIS "as a kind of tuning fork," its structure retaining the echoes of everyone who'd ever been aboard. As such, the appropriate technology could recreate "any or all of the former Doctors" in corporeal form as long as the requisite energy lasted. So when the present Doctor is incapacitated, he can activate this "memory function" and "seek help from his predecessors." The story would be a battle of wits between the Doctors and an ancient computer which has been drifting for 20,000,000 years. "But I see no Cybermen in it," concluded Holmes.

Following the scheduled meeting on 1 September, Holmes was still uneasy, agreeing to write the story's first 20 minutes but simultaneously nominating other writers to take over the project. Matters came to a head on Wednesday 13 October when Saward and Holmes met to discuss the storyline and sample script pages.

"Bob went off and wrote 14 or 15 pages of the script and I read them and to be honest they weren't very good," recalled Saward. "I don't know what had gone wrong; I mean, they were funny but it was ploddy and it was as if his heart was not really in it."

Saward was right, as was proved when Holmes asked to be released from the project. "I couldn't see any way of

accommodating their requirements (five Doctors, companions, the Master, and so on) in one story. So I dropped out," he explained in 1984.

In fact, Saward and Nathan-Turner had already approached another former *Doctor Who* script editor. In due course, Terrance Dicks delivered a script entitled *The Five Doctors*, which would take the Doctors into the Death Zone and the Tomb of Rassilon.

However, rather than waste a good idea, Holmes was able to recycle the notion of the Second Doctor being experimented on by an alien race keen to learn the secret of time travel. On this occasion he would be rescued by his sixth incarnation, and this double-Doctor escapade with the Sontarans duly reached television screens in February 1985 as *The Two Doctors*. ✲

Opposite page: A Cyberman is destroyed by the Raston Warrior Robot in *The Five Doctors*.

Opposite page inset: The Master in the Death Zone, from *The Five Doctors*.

Above: The Master, Sarah Jane Smith, Tegan and the Brigadier (Nicholas Courtney) in the Tomb of Rassilon, from *The Five Doctors*.

HOLMES WAS ABLE TO RECYCLE THE NOTION OF THE SECOND DOCTOR BEING EXPERIMENTED ON BY AN ALIEN RACE KEEN TO LEARN THE SECRET OF TIME TRAVEL.

Left: Some of Holmes' ideas for *The Six Doctors* resurfaced in *The Two Doctors* (1985), starring Patrick Troughton and Colin Baker.

Above: The Sontaran Varl (Tim Raynham) in Part Three of *The Two Doctors*.

"I FEEL ALMOST AS THOUGH THIS PART WAS MADE FOR ME, OR I WAS MADE FOR THIS PART."

COLIN BAKER

The Sixth Doctor's television tenure was all-too-brief, but proved to be just the beginning of Colin Baker's association with his most famous role.

FEATURE BY **DAVID MILLER**

Hard-working, unpretentious, old-school – these are the characteristics that have helped Colin Baker's acting career last for more than 40 years. Back in 1984, he became the Sixth Doctor in an explosive regeneration sequence in which director Graeme Harper took a cue from the cacophonous crescendos of the Beatles' track *A Day in the Life*. It now seems an entirely appropriate start to Baker's time on the programme, which was to be as dramatic behind the scenes as it was on screen.

His first appearance in *Doctor Who*, however, was in Peter Davison's second season. The story *Arc of Infinity* (1983) was set on the Time Lords' planet of Gallifrey; as Guard Commander Maxil, Baker had to shoot the Doctor at Part One's cliffhanger. Baker gave it all he'd got, pointing out that "I've never been one to regard a small part as a small part." Producer John Nathan-Turner appreciated this hell-for-leather attitude, but nevertheless asked him to rein Maxil in a bit.

A little later Baker joined some of the *Arc of Infinity* crew, including Nathan-Turner, at the wedding of assistant floor manager Lynn Richards. At the reception Baker was on top form, regaling the other guests with a stream of funny anecdotes and impersonations, and Nathan-Turner was convinced that if the actor could entertain this showbusiness crowd, he could certainly make something of the role of the Doctor.

"I allowed myself a good 12 seconds before accepting the part," said Baker. "It's everyone's dream to play their hero, whether it's Lancelot or Biggles or Doctor Who. I feel almost as though this part was made for me, or I was made for this part."

Colin Baker was born in London on 8 June 1943, during an air-raid. After the war his family moved to Rochdale and Baker attended St Bede's College in Manchester. Although interested in amateur dramatics, he went on to study law. But he couldn't quite see himself as a solicitor. "After five years I thought, I've only got one life, I'll have a go at doing what I want to do."

He attended the London Academy of Music and Dramatic Art (LAMDA) for three years, studying alongside David Suchet. After graduating, Baker worked in the theatre prior to making his first television appearance in 1970 in a BBC2 serialisation of Jean-Paul Sartre's *Roads to Freedom*. His flamboyance and elegant diction suited the classics and there were further TV roles in adaptations of Balzac's *Cousin Bette* (1971), with Helen Mirren, and Tolstoy's *War and Peace* (1972).

From 1974, Baker played merchant banker Paul Merroney in three seasons of the BBC's family saga *The Brothers*, becoming a tabloid favourite as 'the man you love to hate'. Liza Goddard was cast as April, Merroney's secretary, in 1976. The pair fell in ▷

Above: A portrait from Colin Baker's first *Doctor Who* photocall, on 19 August 1983.

Opposite page: "I am the Doctor, whether you like it or not." A publicity shot of Baker as the Sixth Doctor from his first story, *The Twin Dilemma* (1984).

Below left: Baker as Commander Maxil, alongside Paul Jerricho as the Castellan, in *Arc of Infinity* (1983).

Below right: Baker as Anatole Kuragin, with Morag Hood as Natasha Rostova, in a 1972 episode of *War and Peace*.

"WHY DOES THE DOCTOR NEED A *COSTUME*? WHY CAN'T HE JUST WEAR CLOTHES?"

Top: Baker and Liza Goddard in a 1976 episode of *The Brothers*. The couple later married.

Top right: "Change my dear" – a publicity shot from the first episode of *The Twin Dilemma*.

Above: Behind bars in *Vengeance on Varos* (1985).

Right: On location in Spain with Patrick Troughton, Frazer Hines and Nicola Bryant, during rehearsals for *The Two Doctors* in August 1984.

love and were married that year, both on screen and off. Goddard later remarked that she and Colin "were great friends, but should never have married." They divorced in 1978.

Finding himself typecast by *The Brothers*, Baker returned to the stage, together with occasional television appearances that included a barnstorming turn in *Blake's 7*.

He also married actress Marion Wyatt and fathered four children. In early 1984, shortly before Baker's first appearance as the Doctor, the couple's baby son Jack died from Sudden Infant Death Syndrome. Baker threw himself wholeheartedly into fundraising for research into the condition.

When Peter Davison announced his decision to leave *Doctor Who*, John Nathan-Turner told the press that he was looking to cast someone "more eccentric, much older." (*The Sun* suggested the departing Labour leader Michael Foot.) To counter the Fifth Doctor's affable charm, it was decided to make the new Doctor more unsettlingly alien, prone to violent rages, narcissism and moping self-pity. Baker – who, at 40, was only seven years older than Davison – was aware that "we needed to wrong-foot the viewer", but concedes that this controversial decision initially made the character difficult to accept.

The Doctor's fractured persona was echoed in Baker's costume, devised by Nathan-Turner as "totally tasteless", supposedly to show the Doctor's alien sensibilities but with more than a nod to the garish Hawaiian shirts the producer himself favoured. Baker, who had envisaged a costume in priestly black, was quietly dismayed. "Why does the Doctor need a *costume*?" he asked later. "Why can't he just wear clothes?"

Baker's début at the end of Davison's third season was low-key, with press reaction muted but generally positive. Through the summer, he made public appearances as the Doctor and was given an encouragingly warm reception. His first full season in January 1985 started well, though the second story *Vengeance on Varos*, an intelligent parable about TV violence, caused an outcry over its 'horror' scenes.

Patrick Troughton and Frazer Hines returned for *The Two Doctors*, which boasted location filming in Spain. Ratings were good and Baker was winning over more fans.

Then things ground to a shuddering halt with the leaked news that the series was going to be cancelled, part of a plan to save £2 million by BBC

One Controller Michael Grade. (The cost of a 45-minute *Doctor Who* episode was given as £180,000.) Baker told the press that he was "staggered and disappointed" by the news. "If I were an ordinary member of the public I would express my rage much more than I am allowed to do," he said. The BBC, overwhelmed by the public response in support of the show, commuted the sentence to an 18-month postponement, keeping Baker under contract.

Doctor Who returned in the autumn of 1986 with a 14-part adventure, *The Trial of a Time Lord*, but controversy still dogged the show. Though the series was granted another season in 1987, Grade called for Baker to be replaced. The actor stepped down with a good deal more decorum than might have been expected under the circumstances, but declined to return for a regeneration story.

Never one to look back, Baker returned to the stage with great success, his personal highlights including a run in *Privates on Parade* as drag artist Terry Dennis. Other plays included *Deathtrap*, *She Stoops to Conquer* and *The Woman in White*, and in late 2010 he played Colin Dexter's Inspector Morse in *House of Ghosts*.

Since 1995, Baker has written a weekly column for the *Bucks Free Press* newspaper, and has also mucked in for a number of TV quizzes and reality shows. In November 2012 he bedded down in the Australian jungle for the 12th series of *I'm A Celebrity... Get Me Out of Here!* but was home in time to play the Dame in *Sleeping Beauty* at the Bournemouth Pavilion.

And, of course, Baker has never really left *Doctor Who*. He excelled as the Doctor in the 1989 stage production *The Ultimate Adventure*, inheriting the lead role from Jon Pertwee, then took part in a number of unofficial, *Who*-flavoured video dramas with his former co-star Nicola Bryant.

Baker has also starred in more than 60 *Doctor Who* audio adventures for Big Finish, revelling in the opportunity to tell stories without budgetary constraints and making the Doctor a gentler, more sympathetic figure. Many fans cite Baker as the very best of the audio Doctors.

Indeed, he's welcomed by admirers at conventions all over the world. His raconteur's powers undimmed, he can still hold an audience in the palm of his hand. ✳

Top: "Look to your own predicament, Doctor." At the mercy of the Valeyard – as well as the BBC – in Part Thirteen of *The Trial of a Time Lord* (1986).

Above: In 1989 Baker returned to the role of the Doctor, alongside Judith Hibbert as Delilah, in the stage play *The Ultimate Adventure*.

Right: As Desmond Dewhurst in *The Knock* (1997).

OTHER ROLES

COUSIN BETTE (1971)
With pencil moustache and hair artfully crimped, Baker simpered magnificently as the aesthetic, artistically inclined Count Wenceslas Steinbock, who becomes caught up in the amorous machinations of Helen Mirren's seductive Valerie.

WAR AND PEACE (1972)
Baker played lusty soldier Anatole Kuragin in the BBC's 20-episode serialisation. Anthony Hopkins co-starred as Bezukhov. The pair share a spectacularly energetic fight sequence, with Kuragin given a good thrashing for his advances on the lovely Natasha Rostova.

THE BROTHERS (1974-76)
Baker described his character in this big BBC hit – ruthless banker Paul Merroney – as a kind of 'prototype JR Ewing'. Kate O'Mara co-starred, later joining Baker to spar once more as the Rani in *Doctor Who*.

BLAKE'S 7: THE CITY AT THE EDGE OF THE WORLD (1981)
In this episode Baker played Bayban the Berserker, the second most dangerous man in the galaxy, "with a reputation for straightforward mayhem that's second to none." Resplendent in studded black leather, Bayban comes across like a well-spoken Hell's Angel.

CORPSE! (1987)
One of the actor's favourite stage performances. Co-starring with Jack Watling, Baker actually had two roles, as homicidal twin brothers. The play went on tour for six months then granted Baker the prestige of an above-the-title West End run.

THE KNOCK (1997)
Baker played forger Desmond Dewhurst in four episodes of the long-running (1994-2000) ITV drama about Customs and Excise officers. "Dewhurst was an artist who found it was easier to make money making plates for $20 bills than by painting," said Baker, "he doesn't really get involved in hands-on nastiness." It was Baker's first ongoing TV role since *Doctor Who*.

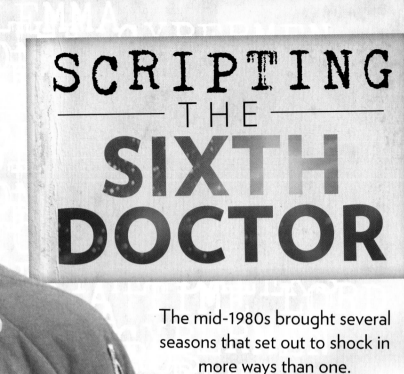

SCRIPTING THE SIXTH DOCTOR

The mid-1980s brought several seasons that set out to shock in more ways than one.

FEATURE BY **JUSTIN RICHARDS**

The stories of the Sixth Doctor are dominated by set-pieces and continuity.

His first story, *The Twin Dilemma* (1984), showcases the Doctor himself, allowing ample opportunity for him to rail against every injustice, real or perceived. The later adventures seem designed to allow for set-pieces of action and drama, often only loosely linked and wrapped around stories that draw heavily on the series' past continuity.

The 18-month break between seasons in this era also forms an obvious divide in narrative terms. The stories that make up *The Trial of a Time Lord* (1986) are tightly bound into a single framework, the continuity coming from within the episodes rather than from earlier years.

But there remains a close interdependence. Understanding the denouement depends on having seen the initial four *Trial* episodes. The ending of the second set of episodes

HE ANNOUNCES HIS PRESENCE IN GLORIOUS TECHNICOLOR EVEN BEFORE HE SPEAKS.

(Parts Five to Eight) is unsatisfactory except within the context of the overall trial and subsequent revelations. Parts Nine to Twelve are the most self-contained, but even these address the possibility that the Matrix is an unreliable narrator. It might have seemed a strange choice at the time but the decision to bring the whole set of stories together under a single title is actually less misleading than the suggestion that the series comprises four separate narratives.

In a similar way, the previous season is more a part of the ongoing story of *Doctor Who* than most. *Attack of the Cybermen* (1985) is a direct sequel to *The Tomb of the Cybermen* (1967), in narrative if not visual terms, with a prerequisite knowledge of *Resurrection of the Daleks* thrown in. *The Mark of the Rani* (1985) continues the Master's story arc, albeit in a looser manner than some of his reappearances. *The Two Doctors* (1985) plays obvious games with (sometimes mis-remembered) continuity, and *Revelation of the Daleks* (1985) continues the story of Davros' attempts to create a new, more loyal race of Daleks.

Only *Vengeance on Varos* and *Timelash* (both 1985) don't follow pretty much directly on from previous stories. *Timelash*, however, brazenly draws on a previous Third Doctor adventure

that was never televised or previously referenced, while *Varos* explores the very nature of a television narrative like *Doctor Who*.

The Doctor himself remains central to the stories; he's the *raison d'être* for *The Trial of a Time Lord*, of course. While the Fifth Doctor was happy to remain in the background unless and until he was needed, Colin Baker's Sixth Doctor is of the opposite inclination. He announces his presence in glorious Technicolor even before he speaks. When he does speak, his dialogue is often theatrical and overblown, frequently at high or increasing volume.

It's almost as if this Doctor wants to shock those whom he encounters. It certainly looks as if the production team set out to shock with the horrific and startling set-pieces that populate and often define these stories. Sinister policemen gun down fleeing prisoners on London streets; the Cybermen not only convert humans into their own kind but torture prisoners, crushing Lytton's hands to a bloody pulp. Again, the series' own past is being raided, as these atrocities echo similar but less extreme sequences in *Terror of the Autons* (1971) and *The Tomb of the Cybermen*. But new horrors are perpetrated in the form of, for example, death by acid bath and a mutating human begging to be killed – similar to a scene

cut from *The Ark in Space*, having been deemed too extreme.

It's a simplistic analysis, perhaps, but the Sixth Doctor's typical story involves him encountering an old enemy who's following through on a previous plan. After a series of well-staged action-horror sequences, the Doctor confronts the villain(s) in a storm of loudly righteous indignation before embarking on a final plan that he predicts will destroy them utterly.

This is a narrative that values shock over logic, in which everything is larger than life and twice as bombastic – starting with the Doctor. And, like the Doctor, there's a feeling that everything is just slightly out of control. ✶

SYLVESTER McCOY

Sylvester McCoy was hired to inject some humour to the role of the Doctor, but ultimately took the programme in a darker direction.

FEATURE BY **DAVID MILLER**

Impish, unpredictable and endlessly inventive, Sylvester McCoy is a unique performer with a career encompassing everything from knockabout slapstick to the monologues of Samuel Beckett.

He lists among his heroes such legendary clowns as Stan Laurel and Buster Keaton, and has explored their work in one-man shows based on their lives. He's played Shakespeare with the greats and has a particular rapport with younger audiences. With his soulful eyes and expressive features, he embodies a kind of indefinable otherworldliness that was a perfect fit for *Doctor Who*. It's the children who watched him as the Doctor who remain among his most devoted admirers.

He was born Percy James Patrick Kent-Smith on 20 August 1943 in Dunoon, Scotland. Like Tom Baker, as a young man he studied to join the priesthood but he left at the age of 16 – when, as he recalls, "I discovered girls." He travelled to London, spurred on by his grandmother's observation that he was "predestined" for the stage.

After a dismal period with an insurance company he joined the backstage staff of the Roundhouse Theatre in Chalk Farm. It was here that he finally emerged as one of the anarchic players in the legendary Ken Campbell Roadshows. He also acquired his stage name 'Sylveste McCoy', coined by fellow Roadshow actor Brian Murphy. Sylveste came from a drinking song about a legendary hero "with a row of 40 medals on his chest" and McCoy from 'the real McCoy' – the genuine article.

McCoy's role as the troupe's cut-price daredevil involved stuffing a live ferret down his trousers and having a six-inch nail hammered up his nose. Some of these early Roadshow antics are preserved for posterity in the 1979 film of *The Secret Policeman's Ball*.

In time, Sylveste became Sylvester and McCoy became a mainstay of BBC children's television, his crazy physicality particularly suited to *Vision On*, a programme aimed at deaf children. He befriended producer Clive Doig and later joined Doig's repertory company in the much-loved shows *Jigsaw* (1979-85) and *Eureka* (1982-86). He also appeared in *Tiswas* (1974-82), ITV's chaotic Saturday morning show.

On film, he can be spotted among the lunatics in John Badham's 1979 version of *Dracula*, while on stage he worked with Vanessa Redgrave and Timothy Dalton in a 1986 production of *Antony and Cleopatra*. A few months later, Dalton had become the new James Bond and McCoy had been offered an equally iconic assignment.

With Colin Baker unceremoniously ousted, producer John Nathan-Turner was once again charged with finding a new Doctor. On the recommendations of Clive Doig and McCoy's agent Brian Wheeler, Nathan-Turner visited the National Theatre where McCoy was starring as the Pied Piper in a children's show written for him by Adrian Mitchell. McCoy's name was added to a list of candidates that also included his old boss Ken Campbell. But it was McCoy who, after a lengthy audition, won the role; he was introduced to the press on 2 March 1987. ▶

Above: Nose job – Sylvester McCoy performs a famous trick with a hammer and nail as part of comedy act *The Ken Campbell Roadshow* in the 1970s.

Opposite page: On location at Barry Island for *Delta and the Bannermen* on 3 July 1987.

Below: Another stunt for Ken Campbell – the fearless McCoy has ferrets stuffed down his trousers.

Below right: McCoy's *Doctor Who* photocall, with Bonnie Langford in the *Blue Peter* Garden on 2 March 1987.

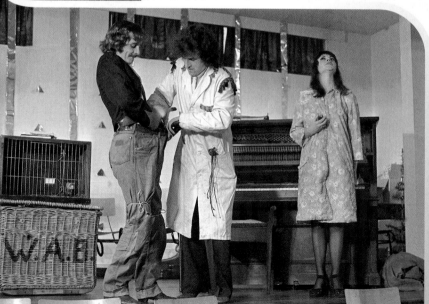

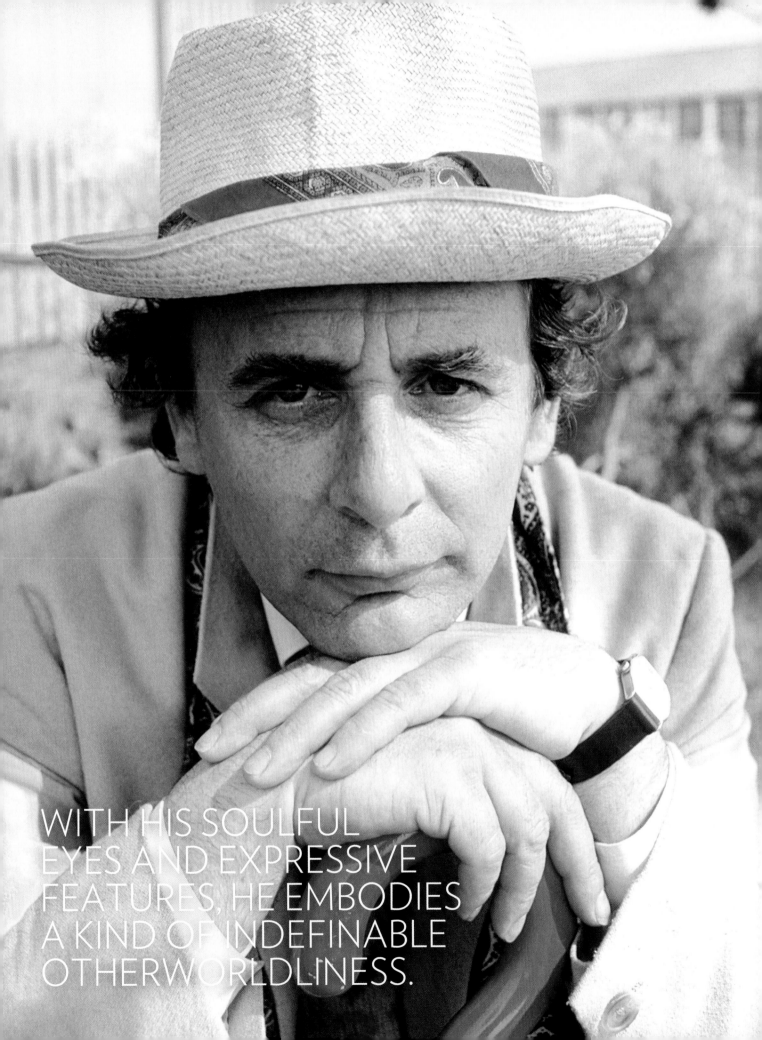

WITH HIS SOULFUL
EYES AND EXPRESSIVE
FEATURES, HE EMBODIES
A KIND OF INDEFINABLE
OTHERWORLDLINESS.

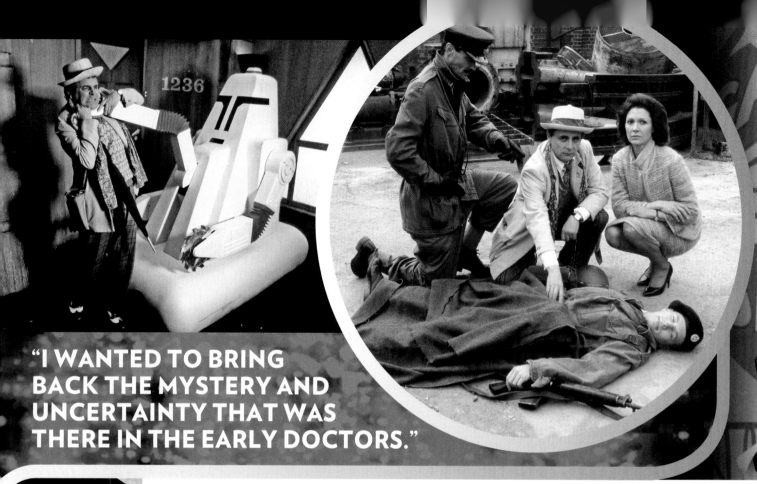

"I WANTED TO BRING BACK THE MYSTERY AND UNCERTAINTY THAT WAS THERE IN THE EARLY DOCTORS."

Top: The Doctor (Sylvester McCoy) discovers that *Paradise Towers* (1987) can be a pain in the neck.

Top right: "His insides were scrambled. Very nasty." The Doctor is joined by Group Captain Gilmore (Simon Williams) and Professor Rachel Jensen (Pamela Salem) in Part One of *Remembrance of the Daleks* (1988).

Above: Joining new companion Sophie Aldred in the *Blue Peter* Garden for her first *Doctor Who* photocall on 13 August 1987.

Right: The post-regenerative Doctor makes a point in *Time and the Rani* (1987).

McCoy was reunited with Bonnie Langford, who was already established as the Doctor's companion Mel. They'd worked together in *The Pirates of Penzance* at the Theatre Royal Drury Lane, when, as McCoy pointed out, "I married her every night... and twice on Saturdays." When Langford left to return to the stage, McCoy was joined by Sophie Aldred as Ace, who quickly became one of the most popular of the Doctor's companions.

Though McCoy's style was brilliantly improvisational, there was no time to accommodate his instantaneous ideas in *Doctor Who*'s strict recording schedule. He was able to make some changes, however. He insisted that the Doctor should never handle weapons and several scripts were rewritten to accommodate this. Then, as he settled in, he found a new direction. "I wanted my Doctor to be darker," he says. "I wanted to bring back the mystery and uncertainty that was there in the early Doctors." He also recalled his 100-year-old grandmother's words about the loneliness that comes with great age.

Working with script editor Andrew Cartmel, McCoy made the Doctor a more enigmatic figure, though he admitted that the task was like "turning an oil tanker." Even so, between them Cartmel and McCoy succeeded in bringing a measure of stability and confidence to the series that had been missing for several years.

The next season included the highly regarded *Remembrance of the Daleks* (1988), which was an electrifying experience for McCoy. "A thrill went round the rehearsal room when one of the Dalek voices first said 'Exterminate!'" he told the *Radio Times*. "The hair stood up on the back of my neck. It was a lovely feeling of fear, like when you're young. I didn't feel I was a real Doctor Who until I was doing a story with the Daleks."

The 1988 season continued with a satire on Thatcherism (*The Happiness Patrol*), the return of the Cybermen for the show's 25th anniversary (*Silver Nemesis*) and a circus story (*The Greatest Show in the Galaxy*) that was partly made in a big top tent in a BBC car park when an asbestos scare closed the studios at Television Centre.

McCoy's third season continued the darker shading of the Doctor's character, presenting some strong stories which many fans now regard as classics. But at the end of the story *Survival*, after the Doctor's climactic struggle with the Master (Anthony Ainley), *Doctor Who* was finally taken off the air. As the Doctor and Ace set off for new horizons, a voiceover by McCoy provided a poignant coda. "Somewhere there's danger, somewhere there's injustice, and somewhere else the tea is getting cold..." The voiceover was recorded on 23 November 1989, 26 years to the day after the first episode of *Doctor Who* had been transmitted.

That wasn't quite the end, however. McCoy's many-faceted Doctor inspired the *New Adventures* novels which Virgin Books began publishing in 1991. Then, in 1996, McCoy returned to *Doctor Who* to hand over the role to Paul McGann in Universal's big-budget TV Movie. McCoy

VISION ON (1965-76)

This innovative BBC series for deaf viewers ran for 12 years. McCoy was a regular in later seasons, usually featuring in mime sequences. Tony Hart painted pictures and Wilf Lunn presented incredible Heath Robinson-style inventions.

BIG JIM AND THE FIGARO CLUB (1979)

This short-lived BBC sitcom, set in a seaside town in the post-war austerity years, saw McCoy as Turps, one of a gang of put-upon builders at odds with the local council's chief of works. McCoy's Roadshow bandmate Bob Hoskins was the narrator.

JIGSAW (1979-85)

In this enjoyably encyclopaedic children's series, McCoy and David Rappaport – 3' 11" tall – played the O-Men, clumsy comic superheroes in long underwear. McCoy maintained that Rappaport would have made an excellent Doctor.

THE LAST PLACE ON EARTH (1985)

McCoy was quietly understated as gentle polar explorer Lt 'Birdie' Bowers in this ITV mini-series. Martin Shaw played Scott of the Antarctic; Max Von Sydow, Hugh Grant and Bill Nighy also starred.

KING LEAR (2008)

An excellent filmed record of the stage hit. As the Fool who watches his beloved King descend into madness, McCoy is powerfully moving and matches Ian McKellen note for note.

THE HOBBIT: AN UNEXPECTED JOURNEY (2012)

Whether he's nursing sick hedgehogs back to life or evading Orcs in his sled pulled by superfast Rhosgobel rabbits, McCoy's turn as wizard Radagast the Brown is a catalogue of delights.

---

gets only a few scenes but looks completely at home in the massive TARDIS set, wearing a spruce new costume that he pointed out was "very *Uncle Vanya*." From 1999 he became a welcome part of the Big Finish ensemble and there was a one-off return to the BBC for an innovative webcast/radio serial, *Death Comes to Time* with Stephen Fry, in 2001.

In 2007 McCoy received the signal honour of being cast as the Fool to Ian McKellen's King Lear, on McKellen's recommendation. The Royal Shakespeare Company production was a sell-out in London in tandem with a production of *The Seagull* featuring the same cast. Both plays were then taken on tour to Australia and New Zealand.

In 2011, McCoy returned to New Zealand to play Radagast the Brown in director Peter Jackson's epic adaptation of *The Hobbit*. Jackson is an avid *Doctor Who* fan and had previously considered McCoy for the role of Bilbo Baggins in his *Lord of the Rings* trilogy; McCoy was also championed by *The Hobbit*'s original director Guillermo Del Toro.

Radagast is a kind of eco-warrior wizard with birds nesting in his hair, his face peering out from a thicket of whiskers. Beneath this disguise it's clear that the Seventh Doctor is alive and well, now living in Middle-Earth. ✻

Top: The Doctor and Ace (Sophie Aldred) outside *The Greatest Show in the Galaxy* (1988).

Above: Handing over to the Eighth Doctor, Paul McGann, in a publicity shot from the *Doctor Who* TV Movie (1996).

Right: As Radagast the Brown in *The Hobbit: An Unexpected Journey* (2012). Peter Jackson, the film's director, has a Seventh Doctor costume in his collection of memorabilia.

SCRIPTING
THE
SEVENTH DOCTOR

The Doctor's seventh incarnation is one of the most calculating and mysterious of them all.

FEATURE BY **JUSTIN RICHARDS**

The Seventh Doctor's universe is one where the action sprawls across time and space.

Scale loses its importance as the Navarino tourists in *Delta and the Bannermen* (1987) are killed off wholesale as soon as they become irrelevant to the plot. In *Dragonfire* (1987) the whole population of Iceworld can be evacuated in minutes (and then also executed for plot redundancy). The events of *Silver Nemesis* (1988) seem to have little effect on the real world – no one pays much attention to Lady Peinforte magically appearing in a tea room, for example. Disappearances in Perivale in *Survival* (1989) elicit only a lukewarm response from the locals... The London streets and playgrounds may seem real, but the characters are representational rather than naturalistic.

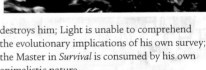

THE SEVENTH DOCTOR'S ERA IS PERHAPS THE MOST STYLISED IN THE SERIES' HISTORY.

The focus remains on the stories themselves, which, though wide-ranging, are never impinged upon by the real world. This works well in artificially created environments like *Paradise Towers* (1987) or *The Greatest Show in the Galaxy* (1988-89). But it sits oddly with more realistic, particularly Earth-based, settings.

The Seventh Doctor's era is perhaps the most stylised in the series' history, and at the heart of this stylisation is the Doctor himself. Sylvester McCoy's Doctor has the wit and wisdom to talk his way out of trouble but often in a non-naturalistic way, as when he talks down the snipers in *The Happiness Patrol* (1988). Similarly, Ace distracts a soldier in *The Curse of Fenric* (1989) with an improbably metaphysical discourse, while a guard in *Dragonfire* happily holds forth on the semiotic thickness of the performed text... The otherwise realistically staged *The Curse of Fenric* ends with a solution to the chess puzzle the Doctor poses for Fenric that doesn't make sense within the context of an actual game of chess.

More than any other, the Seventh Doctor involves himself in the stories in which he's caught up. Often he's not just central but the instigator of the whole narrative. In *Remembrance of the Daleks*, and again in *Silver Nemesis* and *The Curse of Fenric*, the Doctor is playing out the endgame of a plan he set in motion many years, and lives, ago. It's this calculating, almost devious Doctor of later stories that is perpetuated in the Virgin Publishing series of *New Adventures* novels that followed the end of the series in 1989.

A typical adventure of this type sees the Doctor and Ace entering a situation the Doctor already understands and has quite probably precipitated, while Ace is kept in the dark, just as she is in *The Curse of Fenric* and *Ghost Light* (1989). A straightforward goal or objective is complicated by the involvement of different villains with conflicting goals – as in *Remembrance of the Daleks*, *Silver Nemesis*, *The Curse of Fenric*, *Ghost Light*...

Further complication or diversion is offered in the form of a character included largely to provide a guest role for a 'name' performer. And at some point, Ace almost ruins the Doctor's plans through a well-meaning intervention that could have been averted if he had been open with her from the start.

Finally the Doctor reveals that he had the situation under control all along and the villains are hoist with their own petard. The Hand of Omega that the Daleks have been hunting obliterates them; the Nemesis statue the Cybermen seek blows up their space fleet; the Haemovore created and summoned by Fenric destroys him; Light is unable to comprehend the evolutionary implications of his own survey; the Master in *Survival* is consumed by his own animalistic nature...

In other stories, too, the seeds of the villains' undoing are sown into their very character – be it Helen A in *The Happiness Patrol*, Kane in *Dragonfire*, or the Rani in *Time and the Rani*. In a way, this harks back to the earliest and most theatrical dramas – where the main players of Greek tragedy are undone by their own character traits.

Like that early drama, the Seventh Doctor's stories are adventures that take place in a stylised world of heightened reality, demanding that the audience goes along with the non-naturalistic narrative rather than trying to rationalise it. ✳

THE DARK DIMENSION

Doctor Who was no longer in production by 1993, the year of the show's 30th anniversary. But in an unlikely corner of the BBC a bold experiment was under way that could have relaunched the series in spectacular style.

FEATURE BY **MARCUS HEARN** ◆ ILLUSTRATION BY **MARK MADDOX**

"**D**octor Who* is Back!" announced the front cover of *Doctor Who Magazine* in July 1993, and for a while it was a tantalising possibility. More than four years since the studio recording of the final Sylvester McCoy story, it was announced that a new feature-length episode would be produced to mark the series' 30th anniversary.

The Dark Dimension was a co-production between the BBC TV Drama Department and BBC Enterprises (now known as BBC Worldwide). The script was written by Adrian Rigelsford and the director was Graeme Harper. Expectations for the story ran high, but the following month's issue of **DWM** carried the shock news that the project had been cancelled. "We gave it our best shot," said a disappointed Harper. Steve Wickham, co-ordinator of the *Doctor Who* Appreciation Society, told the

kids running a campaign at school to save the environment. They find Tom Baker, worse for wear in a gutter, and get him into the gym. They get him fit and find his hat and scarf so he can once again become the Fourth Doctor and save the environment. This is what they took to Douglas Adams, as far as I know."

Adams reportedly told BBC Video that if they relied on him for a new *Doctor Who* script they'd probably be waiting until the 40th anniversary. Following this genial rejection Vicky Thomas called Nic Crawley, a former colleague at the video distributor Columbia-Tristar. "At that time I was writing a script for Nic called *Scotch on the Rocks*, so Nic recommended me," says Rigelsford. "Vicky called me in and asked if I'd be interested in helping to develop a *Doctor Who* script. Of course I said yes." ▶

> "TOM BAKER WENT TO VICKY THOMAS, THE HEAD OF PUBLICITY, AND ASKED IF IT WOULD HELP BRING *DOCTOR WHO* BACK IF HE RETURNED."

magazine: "We'd hoped that this could have been a new start, but as it's now fallen apart I hope this doesn't mean the death of the programme."

So what *was* this 30th anniversary story? How did it come about, and why was it suddenly cancelled?

The trail of clues begins with writer Adrian Rigelsford. "BBC Video was planning to release *Shada*," he remembers. "It was presented by Tom Baker, who appeared in linking material for the bits that were missing. During the PR for the release in 1992 Tom went to Vicky Thomas, the head of publicity for BBC Video, and asked if it would help bring *Doctor Who* back if he returned. Vicky floated the idea at BBC Enterprises. They realised the 30th anniversary was coming up, and they could probably fund a one-off drama as a straight-to-video release."

David Jackson, head of projects at BBC Video, took charge of the proposal. "The first thing he did was approach Douglas Adams about writing a script," recalls Rigelsford. "Vicky didn't want anyone outside the department to know they were doing *Doctor Who* again, so the one-page pitch document she put together was given the title *The Environment Roadshow*.

"It bore no resemblance to the later script, and was the sort of thing you might see on CBBC now. It was about a bunch of

(Page 0I)

Project Proposal   21/07/1992

Initial Plot Outline : 90-Minute 'Doctor Who' Video Project

~~~~~~~~~~~~   Working title (Environment Roadshow) "The"

Pre-Title Sequence

Christmas Day, 1936. At the height of a violent electric storm, Professor HENRY Hawkspur tapes an audio record of the experiment he is about to carry out, deep in the crypt of a derelict Church.

Using a metalic container unit, shaped like a pyramid, he is attempting to capture and harness raw energy from the static currents of the storm outside, a force which he is certain could provide the power source needed to move through time itself.

He theorises that to be able to travel from one set time period to another, a different dimension would have to be crossed to act as a bridge for the journey. As lightning strikes the pyramid, he's unable to control the energy vortex that is suddenly released within.....

The front of the pyramid implodes, allowing a featureless being to move out of the blinding light within and into reality. It stands, steam billowing off it's form, towering over the cowering Hawkspur.....

– TITLE SEQUENCE –

Storyline

The Future, but not that far away....Christmas.....

Children are starting to disappear across the country without apparent cause or reason; A Child runs from a blazing row between her Parents, retreating to the garden at the rear of her home. Something catches her eye, moving through the woodlands just beyond the garden's boundary.....

As she searches through unending trees, something moves towards her...She turns and screams in horror. We see three Daleks hovering towards her with guns levelled.....

Two boys cycle through a deserted street, with only the moonlight and headlights offering any real illumination. One falls to the ground as the road seems to rumble and shake.... Just in front and behind them, manhole covers over the sewers explode, and Cybermen slowly climb out and start to close in.

A group of school pupils, on a teacher supervised trip,

Scene By Scene Breakdown

Script Revisions - Doctor Who - The Dark Dimension

Sc. 94 – EXT. HAWKSPUR'S MANSION   NIGHT.

THE BRIGADIER and the DOCTOR arrive in Bessie. The DOCTOR gives the BRIGADIER the remote control unit that will activate the vortex. As they drive on towards the mansion, the DOCTOR makes a final check that the BRIGADIER'S sure about how to set up the pylons for the vortex. Bessie passes camera, into...

Sc. 95 – EXT. HAWKSPUR'S MANSION COURTYARD   NIGHT.

We see the BRIGADIER and the DOCTOR by a large statue of Queen Victoria. The DOCTOR tells the BRIGADIER to get on with setting the pylons up, and then heads towards the mansion.

Sc. 96. – INT. HAWKSPUR'S MANSION CORRIDORS   NIGHT.

We see the DOCTOR prowling through the vast, elegant house, searching...

Sc. 97. – INT. RESEARCH CENTRE   NIGHT.

The DOCTOR finds the research centre and confronts HAWKSPUR, taking in the fact that there are two of his future incarnations held there, in cryogenic suspension. The four ECO-TROOPS and ALEX STEWART are guarding ACE and SUMMERFIELD, who are strapped down on operating tables. The DOCTOR challenges HAWKSPUR'S claim that he has the right to destroy the Earth. HAWKSPUR is all to quick to accept a duel – He explains that he no longer needs the DOCTOR alive, as he has the minds of two of his other incarnations to 'Play with'. HAWKSPUR: "If it's a noble death you desire, Doctor...Then so be it!" ALEX STEWART and two of the ECO-TROOPS are left to guard ACE and SUMMERFIELD, while the remaining two guard the entrance to the Research Centre. The DOCTOR and HAWKSPUR'S fight begins...

Sc. 98 – INT. HAWKSPUR'S MANSION   NIGHT.

The DOCTOR and HAWKSPUR fight with their swords as they move up an elaborate stairway...

Sc. 99. – EXT. HAWKSPUR'S MANSION COURTYARD   NIGHT.

The BRIGADIER finishes setting up the pylons in an 8 foot square round the statue. He draws his revolver and sets off towards the mansion, to search for his Son and the others.

Sc. I00 – EXT. HAWKSPUR'S MANSION – ROOF   NIGHT.

The Doctor charges through a doorway, and finds...
(Over.....)

Above: The ideas for *The Dark Dimension* – as distinct from BBC Video's original proposal – started taking shape in July 1992.

Above right: A page from one of Rigelsford's later drafts.

Right: Andrew Skilleter's cover artwork for Rigelsford's 1992 book *Doctor Who: The Monsters.*

Rigelsford completed his initial plot outline for BBC Video in July and began formally negotiating his contract soon after. His book, *Doctor Who: The Monsters*, was published by Virgin that September and was one of the earliest examples of original fiction based on the series' characters and concepts. Rigelsford became a regular visitor to the **DWM** office, and over the coming months the magazine's staff were given privileged glimpses of the story. Rigelsford now admits that what he calls its "timey-wimey" nature makes it seem far from straightforward...

In the future a powerful alien attacks the Earth and wipes out most of mankind. Only the Eco Troops, the last remnants of Earth's defence forces, survive. The Seventh Doctor is dead, killed while creating a trap that sent the alien back through time via an opening in the vortex.

In 1936, Professor Oliver Hawkspur is conducting time experiments that accidentally open the vortex, allowing the creature to escape and take over his body.

By the time we see Hawkspur in the present day, he's become a powerful and ageless businessman. He intervenes in the events at the end of *Logopolis* (1981), capturing the Fourth Doctor moments before he falls to his death from a radio telescope. Hawkspur wipes the Doctor's memory and traps him in a Dark Dimension, preventing his future regenerations from taking place and stopping the Seventh Doctor from ever having defeated him.

As a result of time being altered, Ace now has a completely different existence as a schoolteacher, but carries the memories that the Seventh Doctor transferred to her before he died. Tormented by what she thinks are hallucinations of she reaches out for help from a stranger – Brigadier Lethbridge-Stewart.

Hawkspur loses control of the Fourth Doctor and tries to recapture him using plasma projections that take on the forms of Daleks, Cybermen and Ice Warriors.

The Brigadier tracks the Fourth Doctor to a seemingly abandoned church with a library inside; it transpires that this is all that remains of the TARDIS. Meeting the Brigadier triggers the Doctor's memories and he travels back to 1936 to find out what happened to Hawkspur. Meanwhile, the Brigadier and Ace enter the time vortex in an effort to save future incarnations of the Time Lord before it's too late...

As the script evolved, BBC Video asked Rigelsford to recommend a director. He suggested Graeme Harper, who had been associated with *Doctor Who* in various capacities since 1966 and was acclaimed for his work on *The Caves of Androzani* (1984) and *Revelation of the Daleks* (1985).

"I first met Adrian at a convention in the 1980s and we've remained friends ever since," says Harper. "In 1992 Adrian told me the BBC had commissioned him to write *The Dark Dimension*, so I asked to see it. I thought it was very, very well written, with great dialogue and good voices for each character. It was a really good action adventure that would have worked well even if it hadn't been *Doctor Who*."

The Dark Dimension was to be the first *Doctor Who* story entirely shot on 16mm film since *Spearhead from Space* (1970), and Harper had ambitions to give the story a cinematic quality. "BBC Enterprises intended to package it as a video alongside a book," says Harper. "But Alan Yentob [at that time the Controller of BBC One] had shown an interest in it also being shown on television. As we got nearer production, Enterprises thought that there could also be a theatrical release to play in cinemas. So that's what we were all aiming for."

The team grew with the addition of line producer Nic Nagels and visual effects designer Chris Fitzgerald. In late spring 1993 Fitzgerald read the script and started designing the creatures and Eco Troops. There was no objection from

REDESIGNING THE CYBERMEN

Chris Fitzgerald's Cybercommander is a horrifying vision with skeletal features and harpoon talons. It's the most conspicuously bio-mechanical Cyberman since Sandra Reid's original design for *The Tenth Planet* (1966).

"I created several maquettes for *The Dark Dimension* and lots of illustrations," he recalls. "The key one was the Cyberman. I felt it had been a weakness of the series that so many aliens were established at human height. We wanted to give the Cyberwarrior *stature*. The idea was to cast individuals who were 6' 7", 6' 8", and then put them on stacks. The helmets would have lent even more height, until they were roughly between seven and eight feet tall. We really wanted these things to be a total threat.

"There were human elements incorporated into the suits," he adds, "but we wanted them to have a sense of their own biology, from somewhere completely different from man."

Above and right:
An illustration and maquette of Chris Fitzgerald's Cybercommander.
Images © Chris Fitzgerald.

"EVERYONE, INCLUDING GRAEME, WAS VERY KEEN TO EXPAND THE DOCTOR WHO UNIVERSE, TO SHAKE IT UP."

BBC Video, Rigelsford recalls, to using an outside effects designer. "We weren't a BBC Television production, we were a BBC Enterprises production," he points out. "The BBC would have done the practical effects in studio, but we asked Chris to come up with a new Dalek, a new Cyberman, a new Ice Warrior, and the creature that Hawkspur transforms into at the end."

Fitzgerald remains proud of the work he created over the summer of 1993. "Everyone, including Graeme, was very keen to expand the *Doctor Who* universe, to shake it up," he says. "Initially there was a lot of enthusiasm from BBC Enterprises, and I think they realised that the *Doctor Who* they remembered was long gone. We were pushing it towards something more adult and contemporary. They were certainly buzzed up by our initial presentations. They didn't know quite what they were going to get, but they knew it was going to be interesting."

Fitzgerald clearly recalls the ethos he shared with Rigelsford and Harper. "It was called *The Dark Dimension* and we were talking about using as low a light as possible. We were all in common agreement – we didn't just want the children behind the sofa, we wanted the adults there too."

DISUSED RAILWAY STATION

HAWKSPURS MANSION – WOODLANDS LEADING TO MANSION

Right: Two of Rigelsford's location reconnaissance Polaroids from 1993.
Photos © Adrian Rigelsford.

Far right: One of Chris Fitzgerald's designs for the Eco Troops.
Image © Chris Fitzgerald.

Below: Fitzgerald's redesigned Ice Warrior.
Image © Chris Fitzgerald.

As pre-production continued the script was circulated among potential cast members. Pressure mounted for the story to become more of a multi-Doctor extravaganza in the spirit of *The Three Doctors* and *The Five Doctors*. Why then did Rigelsford make the controversial decision to give the lion's share of the action to the Fourth Doctor?

"Because that was the brief," he replies matter-of-factly. "The BBC gave us a fairly free hand, but they said they wanted Tom as the main lead, with Sylvester McCoy, Sophie Aldred [as Ace] and Nicholas Courtney [as the Brigadier] in peripheral roles. No other Doctors were mentioned. Much later Tom said that he didn't think it would be fair unless the other Doctors were in it as well. The BBC agreed, so I had to add Doctors Five and Six to the script. I'd already added the Third Doctor to an earlier draft; he appeared in a kind of dream sequence as the conscience of the Fourth Doctor."

Frustrated by this relatively limited role, Third Doctor Jon Pertwee later became one of the script's most vociferous critics. "Yeah, there was lot of flak," says Rigelsford with a degree of resignation. "But I don't think

on Tom Baker's Doctor, and because of that we had a few problems signing up some of the other surviving Doctors. They felt it should have been more of an ensemble piece and, you know what, by the time it was made that's probably how it would have ended up."

There was considerably less debate surrounding the casting of the story's villain. "Adrian and I both really wanted Rik Mayall to play Hawkspur," says Harper. "We never got as far as signing Rik up, but he was certainly approached and

PRESSURE MOUNTED FOR THE STORY TO BECOME MORE OF A MULTI-DOCTOR EXTRAVAGANZA IN THE SPIRIT OF *THE THREE DOCTORS* AND *THE FIVE DOCTORS*.

Jon was that well at the time. Although the enthusiasm was there to do a huge amount of action I was told that we had to limit him to scenes where he was sitting down."

Had Tom Baker placed any stipulations on appearing? "A few," says Rigelsford. "He said he was only ever going to do one, and he said he wanted his Doctor to have a heroic death – to have a reason to die. I don't think he was completely happy with his final story, *Logopolis*, so part of the drive behind this was to give his Doctor a better send-off."

Harper also recalls the negotiations that took place with potential cast members. "The story really centred

he was very excited about doing *Doctor Who*. I'd worked with him on *The New Statesman* so he knew me very well and we definitely wanted to work together again."

Unfortunately it was not to be. Shortly after the **DWM** article was published Rigelsford heard that trouble was brewing at BBC Enterprises. "On the Wednesday [7 July] they held an emergency meeting when it became apparent that the funding wasn't entirely there," he remembers. "I was asked to rework the script in order to reduce the budget. Graeme and I stayed at BBC Enterprises until something like quarter past one in the morning. When I got home I continued working, and a courier collected the revised script the next day.

"By Thursday evening I was getting phone calls saying that things were getting a bit hairy, but Graeme and Nic Jagels were confident that everything would be all right. On Friday morning I got a phone call from Graeme saying that we were dead in the water. Penny Mills, who was the senior producer alongside David Jackson, said that we had to shut down. It wasn't a surprise. After the events of the last few days I could see it was heading that way."

HAWKSPUR'S MANSION - FRONT VIEW
MAIN ENTRANCE

HAWKSPUR'S MANSION - CORRIDOR JUST
INSIDE MAIN
ENTRANCE

ABANDONED GRAVEYARD/CHURCH

ABANDONED CHURCH/GRAVEYARD

WASTELAND/WILDERNESS/BATTLEFIELD

TILLARY HOUSE (BRIGADIER'S HOME)

HAWKSPUR'S MANSION - FRONT VIEW

HAWKSPUR'S MANSION - SIDE VIEW
MAIN ENTRANCE

In subsequent years there were rumours that Philip David Segal, the producer of the 1996 *Doctor Who* TV Movie, had asked the BBC to drop *The Dark Dimension* as it was an obstacle to him getting his own film made. "That's not what happened at all," says Rigelsford. "*The Dark Dimension* floundered because of a miscalculation. It came down to a simple mistake on a budget sheet. They wouldn't have made the profit they thought they would."

"I was gutted when I heard the news," says Chris Fitzgerald. "I think a lot of people were frustrated, and not just the people who were working on it. A lot had already leaked to the press, and I think there was an audience waiting to see something new. They were let down more than we were, in a way. In this business you know that things sometimes fall through; sometimes people can't make ends meet and you have to walk away. We moved on to the next project, but it was tough that the fans had got a whiff that it was happening."

Since 1993 Fitzgerald has continued his busy career in visual effects, with credits on the Henson series *Farscape* (1999-2003), the *Harry Potter* films and 2010's *Clash of the Titans*. Graeme Harper has, of course, been a prolific *Doctor Who* contributor since the series' 2005 revival, directing such acclaimed episodes as *The Stolen Earth/Journey's End* (2008) and *The Waters of Mars* (2009).

"No matter what you may hear or read elsewhere, the script for *The Dark Dimension* was a very fine piece of work," he says. "It's a fabulous story, and with the experience I've had of *Doctor Who* I promise you it stands up with the best of them. It would be good if someone read it and decided, you know what, Graeme Harper's right – this would be worth doing. But I doubt whether that will happen now. Maybe it could be made for radio."

Rigelsford's latest project, the script he co-wrote with Helen Solomon for the horror film *The Seasoning House* (2012), is far removed from anything he optimistically dreamt up for *Doctor Who* 20 years ago. He's aware that The *Dark Dimension*, latterly known by the BBC as *Lost in the Dark Dimension*, is still the subject of speculation among fans. He has ambitions to one day publish his script as part of a book describing his experience.

"I've got three major regrets," he says. "The first is that we didn't get to see Graeme's *Doctor Who* movie, and the second is that Tom Baker didn't get to come back as he wanted to. My third regret is that Chris' monsters didn't get seen.

"Despite all that, one of my favourite memories is of something that happened shortly after we got canned. I got a phone call from Nick Courtney, who had been looking forward to playing the Brigadier again. He said it was such a shame, as he'd just started to grow the moustache back!" ✳

Above: More of Rigelsford's reconnaissance Polaroids. The location for Hawkspur's mansion was going to be the Royal Holloway College in Egham.
Photos © Adrian Rigelsford.

Left: Tom Baker finally returned to the role of the Fourth Doctor later in 1993 – with a cameo in the *Children in Need* Special *Dimensions in Time*.

HE HAS TECHNICALLY
BECOME THE FOURTH
MOST PROLIFIC DOCTOR.

PAUL McGANN

After a one-off TV movie, the Eighth Doctor seemed consigned to obscurity. But nine years later he was back in a *Doctor Who* radio series... and it was about time.

FEATURE BY **CHRIS BENTLEY**

"**S**ylvester McCoy now calls me the George Lazenby of Time Lords," said Paul McGann in 1996, shortly after the broadcast of the *Doctor Who* TV Movie. Referring to Lazenby's sole performance as James Bond in *On Her Majesty's Secret Service* (1969), McGann was predicting that his appearance as the Eighth Doctor would be largely forgotten.

Yet McGann went on to flesh out his portrayal in audio adventures for Big Finish and an official animated webcast before starring in an ongoing *Doctor Who* series for BBC Radio 4 Extra (formerly BBC7), bridging the gap between the original run and the revival of the television series.

Combining stories premièred on radio with radio versions of existing audio dramas, McGann has now appeared in 60 episodes, comprising 31 adventures, since August 2005. Despite his single television appearance, he has technically become the fourth most prolific Doctor – after Tom Baker, Matt Smith and David Tennant – in terms of free-to-air broadcast stories.

Born in Kensington, Liverpool, on 14 November 1959, the young McGann aspired to be an athlete, but after exhibiting acting talent in school plays he was encouraged to enrol at RADA. He made his professional début in 1981, appearing as Beatles guitarist George Harrison in Willy Russell's *John,*

Paul, George, Ringo... and Bert at the Haymarket Theatre in Basingstoke. He then starred with his brothers Joe, Mark and Stephen in the 1982 West End musical revue *Yakity Yak!*

That year he also made his television début in a BBC *Play for Today*, *Whistling Wally*, but his big break came in 1983 with the lead in *Gaskin*, a dramatisation of the true story of a mentally handicapped man who fought to be allowed access to his social services file. Next, McGann was cast as snooker player Mo Morris in the comedy drama *Give Us a Break*, his first series role. ▶

SCRIPTING THE EIGHTH DOCTOR

Paradoxically, there are more Eighth Doctor stories than for many of the other incarnations of the Time Lord. But only one of them was televised, which makes defining a typical Eighth Doctor story problematic.

The switch to film from a videotaped mix of location and studio makes for an obvious contrast between the TV movie *Doctor Who* (1996) and what came before it. But if the movie had given rise to a series, then there are clues within the narrative as to how it might have been shaped.

Perhaps the opening narration of the TV Movie would have been retained as a standard way of introducing each story. A narrative arc exploring the Doctor's allegedly half-human background seems likely. In his one television appearance this most human of Doctors faces a very personal threat – a one-to-one battle against his oldest friend and enemy where the Doctor could win or lose the whole world as well as himself.

It would have been interesting to see this Doctor in other settings, opposing more varied threats and villains. But whatever the stories, the Doctor would have been central. This is a hero-driven narrative, with distinct 'moments' of character definition – when he declares that his shoes fit perfectly, or when he uses a gun to get his own way by threatening not to shoot the policemen but *himself*.

The ensuing books, audio plays and comic strips all adhere to an interpretation based on this one story. We shall never know whether any of them take the Eighth Doctor in a narrative direction anywhere close to what might have been. But they demonstrate beyond doubt that the potential was there.

JUSTIN RICHARDS

Above: Paul McGann as the duplicitous hospital porter Matthew Harris in *Paper Mask* (1990).

Opposite page: McGann as the Eighth Doctor in a publicity shot from *Doctor Who* (1996).

Below left: Taking the lead role as Graham Gaskin in 1983 BBC drama *Gaskin*.

Below: A publicity photo for the TV Movie with Eric Roberts (as the Master) and Daphne Ashbrook (as Grace Holloway).

"WE MADE A PILOT THAT DIDN'T WORK. AND IT DIDN'T WORK BECAUSE IT WASN'T GOOD ENOUGH."

Top left: Making enemies of their own futures – Marwood (McGann) and Withnail (Richard E Grant) in *Withnail and I* (1987).

Top right: The Doctor sets the TARDIS controls for Earth, 1999.

Above: "You have to get me out of here before they kill me again!" The Doctor finds a micro-surgical probe left inside his chest during surgery.

Right: With Daphne Ashbrook in a publicity shot for the TV Movie.

In 1984, he appeared as the bisexual Dennis in a successful revival of Joe Orton's *Loot* at London's Ambassador's Theatre, sharing the stage with Leonard Rossiter. Boosting his profile yet further, he then starred as First World War deserter Percy Toplis in Alan Bleasdale's 1986 serial *The Monocled Mutineer*, which brought him a Best Actor BAFTA nomination.

His feature film début came as the anxiety-prone Marwood in *Withnail and I* (1987), cast on sight by writer-director Bruce Robinson. Although the film made little impact on original release, it became one of British cinema's best-loved movies. McGann's performance prompted *The Face* magazine to name him alongside Tim Roth, Gary Oldman and Colin Firth as one of the 'Brit Pack', a group of young British actors tipped for stardom in Hollywood.

Over the next few years, McGann became an increasingly familiar face in British films, with leading roles as a dashing officer in *The Rainbow* (1989), a reckless banker in *Dealers* (1989) and a bogus doctor in *Paper Mask* (1990). Breaking into Hollywood proved more difficult; almost all his scenes in *Empire of the Sun* (1987) and *Alien 3* (1992) were excised before release.

To add injury to insult, he broke his leg while filming the first episode of ITV's *Sharpe* series, forcing his withdrawal from playing the title character and preventing him from working for a year.

In 1994, *Dealers* brought McGann to the attention of Philip David Segal,

executive producer of the American-made *Doctor Who* TV Movie. Initial casting had already settled on Liam Cunningham for the Eighth Doctor but the Irish actor then became unavailable for the planned filming dates. Although McGann was Segal's preferred replacement, production delays meant that it was early January 1996 before he was finally contracted and filming began in Vancouver.

McGann's Doctor was a passionate eccentric with a youthful enthusiasm, a talent for sleight of hand and a willingness to be more open about his heritage, revealing himself as half-human on his mother's side. Resplendent in the clothes of a Victorian showman – a Wild Bill Hickok party costume stolen from a hospital changing room – McGann cut a dashing figure reminiscent of a Romantic poet and seemed born to the part. Yet he'd been reluctant to step into the Doctor's shoes.

"Initially I didn't feel up to it," he told *Doctor Who Magazine* during filming. "I just couldn't see myself in the role. I suppose I just couldn't see the possibilities. In playing the Doctor, it's been hard to find the right level. I spend half the film not knowing who I am, so the character's not even there. I'd like to do more so I can get my teeth into it."

McGann's discomfort wasn't helped by the wig he had to wear. Segal expected McGann to have retained the long hair he'd grown for *The Hanging Gale* the previous

year, but when he arrived in Vancouver McGann had recently had a crew cut for his role as SAS officer Chris Ryan in the ITV film *The One That Got Away*. At short notice, and at a cost of $10,000, Segal had a pair of wigs made from hand-sewn human hair. McGann hated them.

"You know I could have played it as a skinhead?" he said in 2005. "It could have been great. As it was, it was tiresome. You don't want something stuck to your head. It cramps your style."

Aired in the UK on 27 May 1996, the TV Movie attracted over nine million viewers, but its earlier North American screening on the 14th had clashed with a pivotal episode of popular sitcom *Rosanne* and failed to find a significant audience. "We made a pilot that didn't work," McGann told *The Independent* in 2006. "And it didn't work because it wasn't good enough."

Undaunted, McGann went on to lead roles in *Our Mutual Friend* and *Fish* for the BBC, appeared in the feature films *Fairytale: A True Story* (1997) and *Queen of the Damned* (2002), guest-starred in *Poirot*, *Marple* and *Sea of Souls*, and was acclaimed for his portrayal of Lieutenant Bush in ITV's *Hornblower* series. More recently he has been seen in *Luther*, *New Tricks* and *Ripper Street*.

He returned to *Doctor Who* in 2000 to record new full-cast audio dramas for Big Finish, initiating a popular range of Eighth Doctor stories that continues to the present day. In 2005, some of these productions were adapted for radio broadcast to accompany the new television series. Their success prompted the commissioning of an ongoing *Doctor Who* radio series, with McGann joined by Sheridan Smith as northern teenager Lucie Miller. The most recent run of episodes concluded on Radio 4 Extra in January 2013.

McGann welcomed the opportunity for his Doctor to become more integral to the accepted canon. "The Eighth Doctor was one TV appearance, so by volume there's rather little to go on," he told *Vortex* in 2010. "But he's there in the pantheon – he's even reappeared in flashback on some of the new TV stuff.

"It's nice to know that the Eighth Doctor is still part of things and I think there's plenty to come. That's the beautiful nature of the character and the programme: it's never over. Where there's life there's hope." ✳

Top: "So where's the Master?" The Doctor, Grace and Chang Lee (Yee Jee Tso) discover the TARDIS has indigestion.

Above: The Eighth Doctor adopts a new look for the Big Finish audio series *Dark Eyes*.

Right: Bush (McGann) and Hornblower (Ioan Gruffudd) are reunited aboard the *Hotspur* in *Loyalty*, a 2003 episode of ITV's *Hornblower* series.

OTHER ROLES

WITHNAIL AND I (1987)
In his first film, McGann perfectly complemented Richard E Grant's outré drunkard. The pair played 'resting' actors, holidaying in Cumbria by accident during the final days of their friendship.

ALIEN 3: SPECIAL EDITION (1992/2003)
Fourth billed but almost entirely cut from the film's theatrical release, McGann's remarkable performance as Golic, mentally disturbed inmate of the Fury 161 prison facility, was completely reinstated for the 2003 Special Edition.

OUR MUTUAL FRIEND (1998)
This acclaimed six-hour dramatisation of Dickens' last completed novel saw McGann in fine form as moustachioed barrister Eugene Wrayburn, rival to Bradley Headstone (David Morrissey) for the affection of Lizzie Hexam (Keeley Hawes).

HORNBLOWER: MUTINY/RETRIBUTION (2001)
McGann joined ITV's sumptuous seafaring series as Hornblower's faithful companion and best friend William Bush. Here the pair met for the first time, their friendship cemented by harrowing events aboard *HMS Renown*.

JONATHAN CREEK: THE JUDAS TREE (2010)
Not the best of the series' special episodes, although McGann's sympathetic portrayal of vengeful crime writer Hugo Doré was compelling. The main attraction was the opportunity to see McGann on screen with his *Doctor Who* radio companion Sheridan Smith.

WAKING THE DEAD: WATERLOO (2011)
McGann was truly terrifying as corrupt Assistant Chief Constable Tony Nicholson, a man who'll stop at nothing to protect the identity of a sadistic serial killer, in the final episode of this long-running crime drama.

ECCLESTON'S NAME IMMEDIATELY DISPELLED THE IDEA THAT THE NEW *DOCTOR WHO* WOULD BE MERE LIGHT ENTERTAINMENT.

CHRISTOPHER ECCLESTON

One of television's most highly respected actors added extra credibility to the relaunch of *Doctor Who* in 2005.

FEATURE BY **CHRIS BENTLEY**

When the news broke on 26 September 2003 that *Doctor Who* was returning to television, a frenzy of casting speculation gripped the British press. Rowan Atkinson, Eddie Izzard, Jonny Wilkinson and even magician Paul Daniels were among the names being touted for the Ninth Doctor.

Producer Phil Collinson recalled, "We all very quickly realised that whoever we were going to cast needed to be an actor with gravitas and stature and somebody who was primarily known for their drama work. We wanted people to see that this was a drama. The name we kept coming back to was Christopher Eccleston."

Known for his brooding intensity in hard-hitting social and political dramas, Eccleston's name immediately dispelled the idea that the new *Doctor Who* would be mere light entertainment. Yet his involvement was surprising given that he'd previously taken himself out of the running to play the Doctor in the 1996 TV Movie.

"Years ago, when they did the film, I was asked by my agent whether I'd want to audition," he told *Doctor Who Magazine* in 2004. "I said no, very strongly, because I felt then that I wasn't established enough, and I didn't want to be associated with a 'brand name' that early in my career."

Eccleston was born on 16 February 1964 in the Pendlebury area of Salford, Lancashire. Discovering a talent for drama at sixth-form college, he enrolled in a performance course at Salford Tech and completed his training at London's Central School of Speech and Drama.

He made his professional début in April 1989 as poker-playing Pablo Gonzales in *A Streetcar Named Desire* at the Bristol Old Vic. A string of theatre roles followed before his first television appearance, an uncredited part in a Christmas episode of ITV's *The Ruth Rendell Mysteries*.

Soon Eccleston was guesting in episodes of *Casualty*, *Inspector Morse*, *Chancer*, *Boon* and *Poirot*. He also took the lead in his first feature film, *Let Him Have It* (1991), portraying Derek Bentley in the true story of the epileptic teenager who was controversially convicted and hanged in 1953.

Eccleston achieved wider recognition in 1993 as DCI David Billborough in Jimmy McGovern's *Cracker* series. For Eccleston it was the start of a fruitful association with both McGovern and Michael Winterbottom, director of the opening story, but after ten episodes he asked to be written out. He then adopted a Scots accent to play chartered accountant David Stevens in director Danny Boyle's first feature *Shallow Grave*, the most commercially successful British film of 1995.

Boyle's early involvement with *Our Friends in the North* led to Eccleston being cast as tragic drifter Geordie Peacock in Peter Flannery's epic ▶

"IT'S LIKE A VERSION OF ME AS A CHILD, THE WAY I FELT ABOUT THE WORLD AND EVERYTHING IN IT."

Top Left: "If you want the position of God then take the responsibility." Eccleston as Stephen Baxter in *The Second Coming* (2003).

Top right: The Doctor illustrates his proficiency with playing cards in *Rose* (2005).

Above: Jacketless for a rehearsal in the TARDIS set during the recording of *Rose*.

Right: Confronting the Slitheen with a decanter of port in *World War Three* (2005).

drama. After reading the script, however, Eccleston asked to play activist Nicky Hutchinson instead; his performance in the BBC serial earned him a BAFTA nomination and the 1997 Broadcasting Press Guild Award for Best Actor.

His reputation now firmly established, Eccleston went on to a variety of film appearances including *Jude* (1996), *Elizabeth* (1998), *eXistenZ* (1999) and *Gone in Sixty Seconds* (2000), while on television he was seen in powerful productions such as *Hillsborough*, *Flesh and Blood* and a modern-day adaptation of *Othello*. He also received a second BAFTA nomination in 2003 for *The Second Coming*, a thought-provoking religious drama written by Russell T Davies.

When Davies was appointed executive producer of *Doctor Who* later that year, Eccleston contacted the writer to put his name forward for the title role. "I got fixated on this Time Lord," he told *Doctor Who Magazine* in 2004, "and I remember thinking 'He's always moving through time, he's never at home.' That struck me as quite sad really, and also quite resonant for our times: somebody who feels out of place, but also seems to care for human life.

"Then I happened to see *Blade Runner* and I was very, very affected by it. The whole thing with Rutger Hauer's character longing to be human, and all the stuff about whether Harrison Ford's character is human or not. I thought that was very moving, and in some ways it complemented what I'd been thinking about the life of a Time Lord. So I emailed

Russell with my thoughts about it and on the last line of the email I put a PS saying 'If you're ever auditioning for *Doctor Who*, can you put me on the list?'"

He was formally announced as the new Doctor on 20 March 2004. Appearing in Murray Gold's comedy *Electricity* at the West Yorkshire Playhouse in Leeds, he said, "The thing that sticks out for me is the Doctor himself and the mystery of who is he? Where does he come from? What is he thinking? What does he feel? *How* does he feel? He's got two hearts, so does that mean he cares twice as much? He's the idealistic, humane alien and this must be something to do with his desire to belong."

By the time recording got underway on 20 July, Eccleston's thoughts had coalesced into a magnetic performance that combined childlike excitement with dark foreboding and survivor guilt. Eschewing the traditional accoutrements, he created a template for the 21st-century Doctor, dressing casually in black leather jacket and jeans with close cropped hair and speaking with his own Lancashire accent.

"It's the closest I've been to playing myself in a way," he told *Starburst* magazine. "It's like a version of me as a child, the way I felt about the world and everything that's in it. I'm different to all of the previous Doctors in that they speak in RP – received pronunciation. The fact that the Doctor is heroic and very intelligent does say to kids, 'Actually people who sound like this can also be heroic and intelligent.' It's a good message to send."

Eccleston's first episode, *Rose*, aired on 26 March 2005 and was watched by nearly 11 million

OTHER ROLES

LET HIM HAVE IT (1991)

A remarkable feature film début as Derek Bentley, tragic victim of one of Britain's most appalling miscarriages of justice. Eccleston's likable, misguided simpleton made the final scenes almost unbearably moving.

SHALLOW GRAVE (1994)

Three obnoxious friends find their new flatmate dead and decide to cut up the body and bury it in the woods in order to keep his cash. Eccleston's mild chartered accountant was a masterclass in spiralling paranoia.

OUR FRIENDS IN THE NORTH (1996)

As Geordie idealist Dominic 'Nicky' Hutchinson, Eccleston aged from 19-year-old firebrand to grieving 50-year-old photographer. The make-up may be less than convincing, but the performances of Eccleston and his co-stars are outstanding.

28 DAYS LATER (2002)

Eccleston cut a striking figure as Major Henry West, troubled commander of a military outpost which provides unsafe haven during a zombie apocalypse.

THE SECOND COMING (2003)

A breathtaking performance as a Manchester shop assistant who claims to be the Son of God and heralds the arrival of Judgment Day. His "You are becoming gods" speech was sampled for *You Lot* on Orbital's *Blue Album*.

LENNON NAKED (2010)

Though strictly speaking too old for the role, Eccleston was otherwise ideally cast as the self-lacerating Lennon in BBC Four's searching biopic. "It's certainly no whitewash," declared *The Guardian*.

viewers in the UK, the series' largest audience since 1979.

Four days later, the BBC issued a statement announcing that Eccleston would be leaving the series at the end of the current run, erroneously adding that he was tired and feared becoming typecast. Eccleston fiercely objected and within days the BBC issued an apology, admitting that their statement had been falsely attributed to the actor and released without his consent: neither tiredness nor typecasting fears had played any part in his decision to step down.

Departing the TARDIS after 13 episodes, Eccleston returned to theatre work and also tried

his luck in Hollywood with feature roles in *The Dark is Rising* (2007), *GI Joe: The Rise of Cobra* (2009) and *Amelia* (2009). Back in the UK he portrayed John Lennon in *Lennon Naked*, a drugs smuggler in *The Shadow Line*, a corrupt councillor in *Blackout* and an adulterous plumber in Jimmy McGovern's *Accused*, all performances which reinforced his standing as one of the finest British actors of his generation.

He remained silent on his reasons for leaving *Doctor Who* until 2010, when he finally told *Radio Times*, "I was open-minded but I decided after my experience on the first series that I didn't want to do any more. I didn't enjoy the environment and the culture that we, the cast and crew, had to work in. I wasn't comfortable. I thought 'If I stay in this job, I'm going to have to blind myself to certain things that I thought were wrong.' And I think it's more important to be your own man than be successful, so I left.

"But the most important thing is that I did it, not that I left. I really feel that, because it kind of broke the mould and it helped to reinvent it. I'm very proud of it." ✳

Top: Eccleston prepares to record scenes for *The End of the World*, on location at Cardiff's Temple of Peace in 2004.

Above: As Malekith the Accursed – almost unrecognisable beneath an elaborately scarred, pointy-eared prosthetic – in *Thor: The Dark World* (2013).

SCRIPTING THE NINTH DOCTOR

21st-century *Doctor Who* introduced a new pace, economy and emotional literacy to the series.

FEATURE BY **JUSTIN RICHARDS**

Although he was only on our television screens for one series, the Ninth Doctor enjoyed a wide variety of adventures. That one season comprised ten stories – more than the Sixth or Eighth Doctors, and only a couple fewer than the Seventh.

Showrunner Russell T Davies took the time to plan out the stories he wanted for the entire series in his initial format/briefing document. So it's no accident that the first three episodes introduce Rose to the Doctor's universe by taking her from present day Earth to the far future then back to the past. It's a journey that would be repeated to introduce the Tenth Doctor, and again by the Eleventh Doctor with Amy.

THE NINTH DOCTOR'S TIME, MORE THAN ANY OTHER, IS INVESTED WITH EMOTIONAL DEVELOPMENT.

This deliberate breadth of narrative makes it difficult to synthesise a 'typical' Ninth Doctor story, certainly in terms of setting and opponent. But there are elements that recur throughout. Most obviously, the Ninth Doctor retains his Sonic Screwdriver. In the new format, usually telling a single story over a single 45-minute episode, the Doctor's trusty Sonic is key to keeping things moving. Of course, it can't be allowed to become a fix-all, so it has the defined (but vague) limitation of being ineffective against anything protected by a deadlock seal.

Another device introduced to speed up the narrative is the Doctor's Psychic Paper. There simply isn't time in the new structure for the sort of misunderstanding and doubt that was previously almost *de rigueur* in *Doctor Who*. The Doctor needs to be involved and trusted at once. Hence the Psychic Paper allows him access and engenders trust in a moment. Or not. Because, as with the Sonic Screwdriver, there are times when the story demands, either for dramatic or (occasionally) humorous reasons, that it doesn't work.

The straightforward shortcuts of Sonic and Psychic are echoed in the narrative as a whole. Every story has a clear through-line with a well-defined threat. Unlike some of the later stories from the original run of the series, the Doctor's goal is always clear. In the best stories – and here we have ten of them – the audience *knows what has to happen* for the story to end. And in most of these stories, the way the Doctor can achieve this is concrete too. Anti-plastic will deal with the Nestene Consciousness; operating the right controls can save Platform One; the Doctor has a gun that can destroy the escaped Dalek (though he never uses it); Rose's father must die to put time back on track...

But in many of the stories there are complications, not least the emotional price of the solution. This is obvious not only in *Father's Day* (2005) but also when the Doctor has the chance to destroy the Daleks in *The Parting of the Ways* (2005). To do so, he will also have to destroy Earth. The fact that he can't make the same choice as he did to bring the Time War to an end demonstrates how the Doctor has changed through the course of the series.

This change is brought about by Rose Tyler. The Ninth Doctor's time, more than any other, is invested with emotional development. We witness, over these ten stories, the Doctor's humanisation. In emotional and probably moral terms as well, Rose saves the Doctor. In return, he gives his life for her.

But the Ninth Doctor is also a moral force. His disappointment with Adam in *The Long Game* (2005) is rooted in Adam's selfishness – contrasted with the selfless actions of Cathica, which the Doctor himself precipitates. In another recurring narrative motif, he shows her how she can take control of her life and make a decision that saves others. Just as he did with Gwyneth in *The Unquiet Dead* (2005) and as he tries to do with Margaret the Slitheen in *Boom Town* (2005).

All the Ninth Doctor stories have an emotional core. If the solution is technically straightforward, that hardly matters. For the Ninth Doctor, the solution often isn't the most involving element of the story. It's the journey to reach that solution and what it costs himself and his friends. ✳

"I LOVE *DOCTOR WHO* BUT I NEVER EXPECTED TO BE CONSIDERED FOR THE PART."

DAVID TENNANT

An ardent *Doctor Who* fan, and one of the country's most promising young actors, David Tennant's path to the TARDIS might have been preordained.

FEATURE BY **CHRIS BENTLEY**

"**I** was an obsessive, so this is like a dream come true," David Tennant told *Doctor Who Magazine* in 2001. "*Doctor Who* was a big part of why I decided to become an actor, growing up agog at the genius of Tom Baker. Initially I wanted to be a Time Lord, but as I got older that turned into 'Maybe I could be one of the people who *pretends* to be a Time Lord.' And that's what got me into acting."

The date was 26 May, and Tennant was recording his first ever *Doctor Who* role – as the villainous Third Reich officer Feldwebel Kurtz in the Big Finish audio adventure *Colditz*. By the time he became the Tenth Doctor four years later, Tennant had appeared in ten other *Doctor Who* audio releases (notably starring as a superhuman Dalek hunter in the epic *Dalek Empire III* series) and had also made an uncredited cameo as a warehouse caretaker in Episode Five of *Scream of the Shalka*, a 2003 animated webcast.

With hindsight, it's easy to imagine that Tennant was destined to play the Doctor. Two weeks before the relaunch of the television series in March 2005, he appeared on the cover of *Radio Times*, in costume for his lead role in *Casanova* but with a *Doctor Who* strapline positioned next to his head. And on opening night itself, he was the narrator of the preview documentary *Doctor Who: A New Dimension*, shown prior to the first broadcast of *Rose*. Yet when Russell T Davies offered him the role of the Tenth Doctor, it came as a complete surprise to Tennant, who was rehearsing for a live BBC Four broadcast of *The Quatermass Experiment* at the time.

"I love *Doctor Who* but I never expected to be considered for the part," he said in 2005. "When I first got asked I just laughed! I found it hilarious and impossible. I did have a few moments when I wondered if it would be a mistake. And then of course I thought, 'Oh, shut up! Obviously you'll say yes!' What's lovely is that the public seem to have thought, 'Yeah, he'll do.'"

David John McDonald was born on 18 April 1971 – between the broadcast of Episodes Two and Three of *Colony in Space* – in the town of Bathgate in West Lothian, Scotland. At 16, he not only became one of the youngest students at the Royal Scottish Academy of Music and Drama but also made his professional début in an anti-smoking film for the Glasgow Health Board. The following year he appeared in an episode of ITV children's anthology *Dramarama*, adopting the surname of Pet Shop Boys front man Neil Tennant for his stage name.

As David Tennant, he joined the 7:84 Scottish People's Theatre, a touring socialist theatre company, and made his professional stage début in their 1991 production of Bertolt Brecht's *The Resistible Rise of Arturo Ui*. The following year he joined the Dundee Repertory Theatre, appearing in the company's productions of *Tartuffe*, *The Glass* ▶

HE WAS THE POSTER BOY FOR GEEK CULTURE. JARVIS COCKER REIMAGINED AS A TIME-TRAVELLING ACTION HERO.

Top left: With Billie Piper in a publicity image for *The Christmas Invasion* (2005).

Top right: The Doctor makes himself at home at Torchwood House in *Tooth and Claw* (2006).

Above: Tennant as the lovelorn Mr Gibson in *He Knew He Was Right* (2004).

Right: Windblown on the Gower Peninsula while recording *New Earth* in 2005.

Menagerie, Long Day's Journey into Night and *Who's Afraid of Virginia Woolf?*

He was also increasingly seen on television, first in episodes of *Strathblair, Bunch of Fives* and *Rab C Nesbitt* and then in a regular role as bipolar disc jockey Campbell in *Takin' Over the Asylum*. The series got Tennant noticed outside Scotland for the first time and he relocated to London, appearing in a National Theatre revival of the Joe Orton farce *What the Butler Saw*. In 1996 he joined the Royal Shakespeare Company, taking the role of Touchstone in *As You Like It* and going on to productions of *The Herbal Bed* and *The General from America*. In 1999 he appeared as Edgar in an acclaimed staging of *King Lear* at the Royal Exchange Theatre in Manchester and subsequently appeared with the RSC in *The Comedy of Errors, Romeo and Juliet* and *A Midsummer Night's Dream*.

He became more widely recognised, though, for his television work: as Simon 'Darwin' Brown in the ITV comedy *Duck Patrol* and high-profile guest parts in episodes of *The Mrs Bradley Mysteries, Randall and Hopkirk (Deceased)* and *Foyle's War*. He'd already made his first feature film – a brief appearance opposite Christopher Eccleston in *Jude* (1996) – but won his first big screen lead in Mika Kaurismäki's *LA Without a Map* (1998). He was also seen as the repulsive Ginger Littlejohn in Stephen Fry's *Bright Young Things* (2003) and as evil Barty Crouch Junior in *Harry Potter and the Goblet of Fire*, filmed in the spring of 2004 but not released until 18 months later.

Despite considerable exposure over the previous decade, Tennant considers that his breakout role was the compromised clergyman Mr Gibson in *He Knew He Was Right*, the BBC's 2004 adaptation of the Anthony Trollope novel. He followed that with musical murder mystery *Blackpool* and then *Casanova*, a historical romp penned by Russell T Davies with Tennant rising to the challenge of playing the eponymous adventurer. The part was effectively an audition for *Doctor Who*; he was approached to replace Christopher Eccleston before *Rose* even aired.

Introduced at the end of *The Parting of the Ways*, Tennant's first full episode was also the series' first hour-long Christmas Special, *The Christmas Invasion*. Wearing a tight pinstripe suit and sneakers, Tennant's Doctor was dynamic and witty with a youthful enthusiasm tempered only by righteousness and deeply felt loss. Often bespectacled, he was the poster boy for geek culture, Jarvis Cocker reimagined as a time-travelling action hero.

Over the next five years, a further 46 episodes and two animated adventures (*The Infinite Quest* and *Dreamland*) cemented Tennant's status as the series' most popular lead actor – in terms of audience numbers – since Tom Baker. His final episode, broadcast on New Year's Day 2010, was watched by more than 12 million viewers in the UK alone. The event was heralded by Tennant's appearance in over 70 other programmes on BBC television and radio over that Christmas period; he was also seen repeatedly, in character, in specially shot BBC One Christmas idents, shown before every programme on the channel during the holiday fortnight.

Announcing his decision to leave the series, he said, "I love this part and I love this show so much that

LA WITHOUT A MAP (1998)

As a lovelorn Bradford undertaker embarking on a disastrous writing career in Hollywood, Tennant shared a bucket of fried chicken with Johnny Depp (playing himself in an uncredited cameo) and produced a comedy gem.

BLACKPOOL (2004)

Tennant sang, danced and even appeared outside Blackpool's *Doctor Who* Exhibition in Peter Bowker's magical mystery musical. Co-stars David Morrissey, Sarah Parish, Steve Pemberton and David Bradley all later had roles in *Doctor Who*.

CASANOVA (2005)

Romping his way across Europe, Tennant's young Giacomo Casanova was like the Tenth Doctor on Viagra. Russell T Davies' deliciously saucy script was the writer's last work before embarking on the *Doctor Who* revival.

HAMLET (2009)

Showcasing Tennant's brilliant portrayal of the Prince of Denmark as a vengeful but funny manic depressive, this BBC film version of the award-winning 2008 RSC production was the first thing Tennant shot after finishing work on *Doctor Who*.

SINGLE FATHER (2010)

Tennant was outstanding as family man David Tiler whose world is turned upside down by the sudden death of his wife. Co-stars Suranne Jones, Neve McIntosh and Rupert Graves all later appeared in *Doctor Who*.

FRIGHT NIGHT (2011)

As sleazy Las Vegas stage magician Peter Vincent, Tennant became a reluctant vampire hunter with an aversion to shirts in this mildly homoerotic remake of the 1985 vampire-next-door original.

if I don't take a deep breath and move on now I never will, and you'll be wheeling me out of the TARDIS in my bath chair."

Since recording his last scenes as the Doctor in May 2009 – for an episode of *The Sarah Jane Adventures* – Tennant has continued to be as prolific as ever, starring in television dramas *Single Father*, *United*, *Broadchurch* and *The Politician's Husband*, as well as feature films *The Decoy Bride* (2011), *Fright Night* (2011) and *Nativity 2: Danger in the Manger!* (2012). He also returned to the stage in RSC productions of *Hamlet*, *Much Ado About Nothing* and *Richard II*, and somehow still managed to find time to marry his *Dreamland* co-star Georgia Moffett, daughter of Peter Davison.

But Tennant's association with *Doctor Who* is far from over. In April 2013 he returned to Cardiff to reprise his role as the Tenth Doctor opposite Matt Smith in the 50th Anniversary Special, *The Day of the Doctor*.

"I'm coming back onto a show that's effectively somebody else's show and used to be mine – and that's potentially quite a weird situation to be in," he told *Entertainment Weekly*. "Going back to something I knew so well, and had such fun memories of, might have backfired. But actually it felt familiar enough that it was like coming home, and working with Matt proved to be a real joy. It was everything that I hoped it might be." ❊

Above: The Doctor makes a momentous decision in *The Waters of Mars* (2009).

Below left: DI Alec Hardy (Tennant) and DS Ellie Miller (Olivia Colman) question the Reverend Paul Coates (Arthur Darvill) in *Broadchurch* (2013).

Below right: As the eponymous Prince of Denmark in the climactic scene of *Hamlet* (2009).

SCRIPTING THE TENTH DOCTOR

The Doctor's relationship with his companions formed the emotional core of these stories.

FEATURE BY **JUSTIN RICHARDS**

The variety and emotional depth of the Ninth Doctor's era carries through into the Tenth Doctor's tenure, building on the foundations set down in the previous incarnation and playing to its strengths. In narrative terms, we have an even greater variety of stories (of threats, locations, time zones), though still with an emphasis on Earth close to the present day.

The Tenth Doctor continues to be central to his adventures, but the stories are rarely precipitated by him. *Human Nature* and *Utopia* (both 2007), together with the latter's ensuing events, are rare exceptions where the presence of the Doctor is a key factor in igniting the threat that he must face.

Usually, the Doctor, together with Rose, Martha or Donna, arrives in a situation where the threat is already in place and developing. Sometimes the Doctor is summoned or drawn in

Opposite page: "It goes ding when there's stuff." Calling from 1969 with the Timey Wimey Detector in *Blink* (2007).

Opposite page inset: The Doctor helps Professor Yana (Derek Jacobi) to wire up the neutralino map in *Utopia* (2007).

Left: The Doctor and Rose (Billie Piper) arrive at the Crucible space station in *Journey's End* (2008).

Below left: "DoctorDonna friend." The Doctor and Donna (Catherine Tate) are menaced by locals on the *Planet of the Ood* (2008).

Below: The Doctor confronts Son of Mine (Harry Lloyd) in *The Family of Blood* (2007)

MORE THAN ANY OTHER, THE TENTH DOCTOR RELIES ON HIS ABILITY TO TALK HIS WAY OUT OF TROUBLE.

– by the Face of Boe, by Mickey in *School Reunion* (2006), or by Martha and UNIT in *The Sontaran Stratagem* (2008).

More often, the Doctor becomes aware of the threat from his own observations – he sees Lazarus in a television interview in *The Lazarus Experiment* (2007) and learns about the 'ghosts' from Jackie in *Army of Ghosts* (2006). Or he's drawn in by events themselves as they unfold, like the meteoroids hitting the starship *Titanic* in *Voyage of the Damned* (2007).

Depending on how the Doctor first perceives the threat, there may be a period of investigation to clarify the situation. So in *Army of Ghosts*, the Doctor and Rose set up equipment to detect and analyse what's actually happening, while in *Partners in Crime* (2008) the Doctor's investigations of Adipose Industries mirror Donna's own enquiries into the company.

For the first time since the 1960s there are several stories in which the Doctor isn't the protagonist, albeit because of scheduling and production constraints. But even in these he remains the focus. Elton's search for the Doctor in *Love & Monsters* (2006) forms the core of that story. In *Blink* (2007) the Doctor's presence is felt throughout as he advises Sally Sparrow from the past. *Turn Left* (2008) hinges on the

Doctor's absence from the narrative – placing him, paradoxically, absolutely at the heart of the story. The Tenth Doctor is always central and foregrounded.

As with the Ninth Doctor, the relationship between the Doctor and his companion, particularly Rose but also Martha and Donna, forms the emotional core of most stories. The understanding shared by Rose and the Doctor continues to deepen while the Doctor's humanisation is made explicit in a new, more overtly caring and sympathetic incarnation. The enforced parting of Rose and the Doctor forms a narrative thread that extends far beyond the events of *Doomsday* (2006) – prefigured ahead of it, and casting a long shadow over the rest of the Tenth Doctor's time.

But despite being a Doctor who can occasionally show his real emotions, the Tenth Doctor is every bit as determined and ruthless as the Ninth. When he takes this intense, determined morality too far, it can be his undoing – as at the end of *The Waters of Mars* (2009).

Generally this Doctor is in control of events and narrative. His greatest weapons are his wits and his mouth. More than any other, the Tenth Doctor relies on his ability to talk his way out of

trouble. But while words can be his salvation, he can also turn his garrulous, sometimes flippant manner towards sterner stuff. His confrontation with Krillitane leader Finch in *School Reunion* is a pivotal moment not only in that story, but in our understanding of the Doctor himself.

At one point he decries his own lack of mercy, but he's being hard on himself. The Tenth Doctor is willing to give his enemies a chance, going to great lengths to avoid bringing down the short-lived Family of Blood in *Human Nature/The Family of Blood* (2007). But when other avenues are exhausted, when the enemy has ignored the Doctor's offer of clemency, then he is indeed without mercy. ✳

THE DOCTOR, THE DESIGNER AND THE WARDROBE

Each of the Doctors has worn a costume that became synonymous with his character. Some of the designers behind those costumes reveal their inspiration.

FEATURE BY **CHRIS BENTLEY**

Jon Pertwee
'DR WHO' - 'Terror of the Autons'
Black Evening Coat
ruined in Purple Satin (Blue?)
White Frilled Shirt

Fun Coat
progging fasteners

Purple Velvet Smoking Jacket

Black Trousers

Black E/s. Boots.

Left: Ken Trew's redesign of Jon Pertwee's ensemble for *Terror of the Autons* (1971) also appeared in *The Mind of Evil* (1971).

Right: James Acheson modified Pertwee's costume for Season Ten with a green colour scheme first seen in *Carnival of Monsters* (1973). It's modelled here by Pertwee in *Frontier in Space* (1973).

"The apparel oft proclaims the man," declares Polonius in *Hamlet*. Nowhere is this truer than in the field of costume design, where the clothing selected for a character is often a shorthand that offers insights into taste, vanity, wealth, morals, intellect and general state of mind – even if that character is a 900-year-old Time Lord.

Over the last 50 years, the process of creating the Doctor's wardrobe has varied considerably.

The outfits worn by William Hartnell and Patrick Troughton in the 1960s were hired from theatrical costumiers. Jon Pertwee, however, wanted his Doctor to wear a modern-day suit. But by the time filming started on his first story, *Spearhead from Space*, he'd been persuaded to change his mind.

He was closely involved in assembling his ultimate look, as he recalled in 1982. "We'd had a number of dressing-up sessions down in the BBC's Wardrobe Department, and frankly I wasn't really happy with much of what they had on offer. I went home and looked through all the trunks and suitcases that I had of Victorian and Edwardian clothes worn by my grandfather. The capes I took to particularly. I got together what

Above: June Hudson's unused initial ideas for Tom Baker's Season 18 costume, with melton waistcoat and buckskin breeches.

Far right: James Acheson's original costume for the Fourth Doctor, as seen in *Terror of the Zygons* (1975).

I thought was a good outfit, and went back to the BBC and showed them."

As luck would have it, Season Seven costume designer Christine Rawlins had been having similar thoughts. "Around that time there was a series called *Adam Adamant Lives!*" she recalled in *The Frame* in 1990. "Adam Adamant was dressed in period costume, complete with cloak, and I remember thinking that something rather 'romantic' like this would be a good contrast to the previous Doctor. That Jon Pertwee was thinking along the same lines was an agreeable coincidence... Jon was extremely positive and professional and cared very much about the 'look' of the whole production."

Ken Trew subsequently adapted Pertwee's ensemble for *Terror of the Autons* (1971), replacing the original red-lined Inverness cape over a black velvet smoking jacket with a new purple-lined cape over a red jacket. This modification enabled Pertwee to change into jackets and capes of different colours and fabrics from story to story without altering his Doctor's particular style of dress.

"TOM COULD WEAR ANYTHING, BUT HE WAS WORTHY OF THE MOST STRIKING COSTUME BECAUSE HE COULD CARRY IT."
JUNE HUDSON

This approach was maintained for Pertwee's successor, leading to the creation of the most striking and iconic apparel designed for the Doctor to date.

Now an Oscar-winning feature film designer with credits on *Spider-Man* (2002) and *Man of Steel* (2013), James Acheson was the costume designer assigned to Tom Baker's first story, *Robot* (1974-75). "I spent quite a lot of time with Tom," he recalled in 2011, "and I felt that he could wear a hat because he's such a tall man. For some reason I had this image of a Toulouse-Lautrec poster of a cabaret artist called Aristide Bruant in a big floppy hat and a red scarf. I mentioned this to Tom and he kind of went along with it.

"I also wanted to, hopefully, give him *clothes* rather than a costume and I was very keen for it all to be corduroy and rather baggy so that you felt that there were lots of things in his pockets. There were tweedy trousers and brogue shoes but there was this slightly student-y thing with the scarf, and the hat was just a sort of eccentricity. You could change pretty much all of it and luckily, over the following episodes, people did change it and I think it got better: the coat got longer, the waistcoat became a much more structured thing. ▶

THE DOCTOR, THE DESIGNER AND THE WARDROBE

Above: The Doctor and K9 visit Brighton beach before travelling to *The Leisure Hive* (1980).

Below: June Hudson's design for the Fourth Doctor's burgundy costume, rendered in gouache, pencil crayon and pastel.

Bottom right: A replica of Tom Baker's scarf, which was originally knitted by Begonia Pope for costume designer James Acheson. Photo © Helen Solomon.

I think they retained the essence of it but they improved on it."

The Fourth Doctor's costume was adapted a number of times over the course of Baker's tenure but the ultimate refashioning was a stunning burgundy outfit first seen in *The Leisure Hive* in 1980. The Edwardian Norfolk suit with matching hat, scarf, boots and Russian officer's overcoat was designed by June Hudson.

"Tom could wear anything," she says, "but he was worthy of the most striking costume because he could carry it. When I was asked to redesign his costume, I knew exactly what I wanted him to wear and I could see the look of it in my mind's eye; it had to be iconic, it had to be strong and it had to be visible from a distance.

"I liked the idea of it all being one colour and that was very important because I didn't want the image to be cut up. It needed to be a rich, glowing colour, something that would light beautifully, and the spectrum of red was perfect – the colour of fire, energy, nobility and everything exciting. The thing that I think is terribly important about the Doctor is that he's a gentleman, with everything that that implies – nobility, chivalry, courtesy, courage, attraction – and it was that quality that had to shine through.

"One of the major decisions I had to make was about the scarf. As an artist it was a huge temptation to get rid of everything that had gone before and do something completely new, but then I had to consider the programme. Tom used the scarf as a prop and it was part of his personality so I felt we had to keep it, but it would be a transformed scarf. I did it in chenille, a very light material, which has the most beautiful and wonderful colours; those maroon, crimson and plum colours together are lovely.

"I'm thrilled and honoured beyond words to have designed that costume," she says. "For me, designing for *Doctor Who* was the peak of my career. I instinctively knew at the time that it was something special and marvellous to be involved in, and so it has proved."

In the 1980s, producer John Nathan-Turner had very specific ideas about the Doctor's wardrobe. As designer on *Four to Doomsday* (1982), Colin Lavers designed a period cricketing outfit for Peter Davison.

"John had seen Peter at a charity cricket match and decided to bring cricket into the new characterisation," Lavers told the fanzine *Axos* in 1982. "The initial brief was for a morning coat, striped trousers and a collapsible top hat. The hat

"DR WHO"

Tom Baker

June Hudson

> "TOM USED THE SCARF AS A PROP AND IT WAS PART OF HIS PERSONALITY SO I FELT WE HAD TO KEEP IT."
> JUNE HUDSON

was so that the Doctor could produce a cricket ball from time to time. I was against the morning coat and top hat for a number of reasons. The frock coat was my idea. Being single instead of double-breasted, it would be similar to the design of cricket umpires."

Pat Godfrey had the unenviable task of creating Colin Baker's wardrobe when she was assigned to 1984's *The Twin Dilemma*. "I didn't have huge long discussions with John about what he wanted," she recalls, "but he said something which I think ▶

Right: A 1981 publicity photo of Peter Davison in costume as the Fifth Doctor.

Below right: Colin Lavers' proposal for the Fifth Doctor's costume, as first seen in *Castrovalva* (1982).

Below: The costume worn by the Fifth Doctor during Season 21. This was subtly altered by Judy Pepperdine, from Lavers' original design. Photo © Helen Solomon.

Bottom centre: The Sixth Doctor's original costume, designed by Pat Godfrey and tailored by Arthur Davey. Photo © Grahame Flynn.

Bottom right: Grahame Flynn with Sophie Aldred.

Beige frockcoat with scarlet wool trim. Knitted waistcoat. Striped trousers. Lace-up boots dyed beige.

Dr Who 5 S W

COSTUME COLLECTORS

G rahame Flynn amassed an impressive collection of *Doctor Who* costumes and props through friendships with people who worked on the programme, both before and after he became friends with former producer John Nathan-Turner.

In the last few years he has decided to downsize his collection, trading many items so he can concentrate on the highest quality costumes. "If you've got a hundred items you'll never be able to display them all properly," he says. "If you've got fewer items you can display them. In my office I've got a mannequin and I rotate the costumes on it."

Grahame occasionally exhibits his costumes for special events, although he's learned to be vigilant since someone tried to pinch one of his Fourth Doctor's hats. "Somebody distracted me while someone else took the hat off the mannequin," he remembers. "I could see he was about to walk away with it when I stopped him. There are basically only three hats that Tom Baker ever wore in *Doctor Who* and I've got two of them. They're probably worth about £10,000 each."

When the costumes aren't being displayed they have to be very carefully stored. "You need acid-free paper on the coat hangers, and moths are a big problem," he says. "The *Doctor Who* exhibition at Llangollen [which ran from 1994 to 2003] had moths and mice. There was a row of costumes there, including the costume Anthony Ainley wore as the Master, and a mouse went along the rail and ate a hole through the lot."

Grahame's favourite item is an original Sixth Doctor coat from Season 22. "A lot of people hate Colin Baker's costume, but as a piece of work it is divine. It's beautifully tailored. I remember looking at his waistcoat and thinking, I'd love to own that. And now I do.

"I live in a 1930s house which has picture rails. Colin's costume is hanging from one of them and I just love looking at it. It's what I call 'prop art'!"

COSTUME
COLLECTORS

John Walker and Chris Pocock have around 20 original *Doctor Who* costumes in their house. They began collecting monster masks in 2001, but were so disappointed when the Latex rotted that they decided to concentrate on costumes instead. "They're more fun," says John, "and hopefully they won't disintegrate."

John and Chris' costume collection has a very specific focus. "There came a point where Chris and I decided that we could have a mish-mash collection, or hone it down to the era, or eras, that mean the most to us. For me that's the Colin Baker years, and Chris really got into the programme when Sylvester McCoy was the Doctor. From then on we started to sell off anything we had that was a replica, or anything from other Doctors, in favour of getting anything that dated from 1985 to 89.

"As sad as it sounds – and fans will probably tear me apart for saying this – I would love to get one of Bonnie Langford's costumes. Preferably the pink and white outfit from *Time and the Rani* (1987). Four of them must have been made, because Bonnie and Kate O'Mara must have had two each, but if they still exist I don't know where they are. Something else I'd really like is Colin's *Two Doctors* waistcoat, which I know was retained by the BBC at one point."

John thinks carefully before revealing the most they have ever spent on a costume. He sucks the air through his teeth before saying, "We spent £10,000 on each of the Sixth and Seventh Doctors' costumes."

For John and Chris these aren't mere exhibits in a private museum. "We've dressed up many a time," he says matter-of-factly, "but we won't wear them outside the house. I usually wear the Sixth Doctor's costume and Chris wears the Seventh Doctor's. We can't get into anything worn by Peri!"

Above: Colin Baker on the set of *The Twin Dilemma* (1984).

Below: The Seventh Doctor's costume, designed by Ken Trew, with the paisley scarf first seen in *Paradise Towers* (1987). Photo © Chris Pocock and John Walker.

Bottom right: Sylvester McCoy with the original tartan scarf, on location for *Time and the Rani* in 1987.

Bottom left: Chris Pocock and John Walker.

he regretted saying forever afterwards: 'I want a totally tasteless costume.' He wanted it to be 'circus-like' – I can remember that was the phrase that was used.

"I went away and did various sketches and it came together pretty quickly really. It was more the choice of fabrics rather than the structure of the costume, because each new Doctor was a sort of development of the previous one, incorporating bits and pieces so there was continuity. I got loads of pieces of fabric in various colours and played around with them on the work table, putting pieces side by side until I felt they were the right sort of combination."

Previously responsible for the Pertwee make-over, Ken Trew created Sylvester McCoy's look for *Time and the Rani* in 1987. "There was a discussion about what Sylvester was going to look like," he remembers. "John said, 'I want him to look as though you would pass him in the street and do a double take. You would pass him and think, why is he dressed like that?' It wasn't to be as outrageous as Colin Baker's or as grand as Jon Pertwee's.

"Sylvester McCoy came into his audition wearing a Panama hat. About two days later, John said, 'Sylvester is going to do it!' I think that's when the whole thought came through about the Panama hat. The Panama hat was the first part of the costume to be agreed."

In the 21st century, the costume for Christopher Eccleston's Doctor was devised by Lucinda Wright, who discovered his battered leather jacket in a second-hand shop but had his dark V-necked jumpers specially made. Louise Page created David Tennant's brown pinstriped suit entirely from commercially available trousers, buying five large pairs to make up each jacket.

> ## "THE PANAMA HAT WAS THE FIRST PART OF THE COSTUME TO BE AGREED."
> KEN TREW

THE DOCTOR, THE DESIGNER AND THE WARDROBE

"The Doctor"
Simple, stylish anime, help character, not dominate; tough, sleek.

DOCTOR WHO | "The Doctor"
DRW BY: Lucinda Wright | REF CODE
© BBC CYMRU WALES 2004 | DATE DRAWN: May 2004 | D

Battered leather 3/4 Jkt - (900 yrs old).

V-neck jumper (Ep 6 'Green')!

Black trousers - jeans - long + lean for anime.

Colours -
Dark palette -
Deep reds, mauve, tones, dark green; - reflect the Galaxy + stars.

Tough, black leather boots - good for running, Action look.

Far left: Lucinda Wright's costume design for Christopher Eccleston's Ninth Doctor.

Below left: Eccleston relaxes on the TARDIS set during the making of *Aliens of London* in 2004.

Below: Matt Smith's Eleventh Doctor costume, designed by Roy Holman, alongside David Tennant's Tenth Doctor costume, designed by Louise Page.

Left: The Eleventh Doctor (Matt Smith) unmasks Liz 10 in *The Beast Below* (2010).

Designing Matt Smith's costume fell to Ray Holman. "We had to go through tons and tons of clothes," he said in 2010. "I took hundreds of photographs of Matt with different ideas. We had a duty not to repeat any ideas from any of the previous costumes, but we also didn't discount any ideas that popped up during the fittings. We knew we wanted boots; we had the trousers, the shirt, and there were a couple of different coats and jackets."

It was Smith himself, however, who supplied the finishing touch.

"The tweed jacket went on him," Holman recalled, "and we thought, 'That's it!' Then Matt said, 'Can I try a bow tie?'" ✳

Museum quality reproductions of original *Doctor Who* design drawings are available from www.thecollectableartcompany.com

MATT SMITH

The Eleventh Doctor is a maverick in a bow tie who'll march into battle armed with a mop and a Jammie Dodger. Little known when cast, Matt Smith made the Doctor's latest regeneration truly unforgettable.

FEATURE BY **CHRIS BENTLEY**

When Matt Smith's appointment as the Eleventh Doctor was announced on 3 January 2009, the news was met with confusion and consternation. That morning, *The Sun* had confidently named Paterson Joseph as David Tennant's replacement. The news media had apparently never heard of Smith.

'Doctor Who?' asked the headlines next day, as wrong-footed reporters attempted to wring controversy from the decision to cast an actor who was not only 'unknown' but also, at 26, younger than any previous Doctor.

In truth, Smith was a relatively familiar face to discerning BBC viewers who had seen him taking prominent roles in *The Sally Lockhart Mysteries*, *Party Animals* and *The Street*. He was also known to theatregoers for a variety of high-profile performances and had been nominated for the *Evening Standard*'s Outstanding Newcomer Award for his 2007 role in *That Face* at the Royal Court Upstairs.

As for being the series' youngest Doctor, executive producer Steven Moffat described him as "like Patrick Moore trapped in the body of an underwear model."

"I'm really going to work my socks off over the next few years," Smith told *Doctor Who Magazine*. "I'm going to try to make my Doctor as varied, and brilliant, and dark, and unpredictable, and happy, and sad, and funny as I can – every facet of me really – and explore it with bravery and courage. I'm going to do it my way and see where it takes me."

Matthew Robert Smith was born on 28 October 1982 in Northampton and educated at Northampton School for Boys. A promising footballer, he played for Northampton Town, Nottingham Forest and Leicester City youth teams but had to abandon plans to play professionally when he suffered a serious back injury. Taking part in a school production of *Twelve Angry Men*, he began to consider a different career path.

Encouraged by his teachers, Smith enrolled in the Drama and Creative Writing course at the University of East Anglia and also joined the National Youth Theatre in north London. The following year he took the lead in a university production of *Once in a Lifetime* and then played Thomas Becket in TS Eliot's *Murder in the Cathedral*, staged by the NYT at Southwark and Westminster Cathedrals. His appearance in the latter was applauded by *The Guardian*'s Lyn Gardner as "an exceptionally mature performance." ▶

Above: Matt Smith's first publicity photo for *Doctor Who*, taken in late 2008.

Opposite page: The Raggedy Doctor – Matt Smith in *The Eleventh Hour* (2010).

Below: Smith as Jim Taylor in *The Shadow in the North* (2007), with JJ Feild as photographer Frederick Garland.

Below right: The Doctor is caught by Weeping Angels in *Flesh and Stone* (2010).

"I'M GOING TO
DO IT MY WAY
AND SEE WHERE
IT TAKES ME."

VIEWERS QUICKLY WARMED TO SMITH'S ECCENTRIC PORTRAYAL OF A SELF-STYLED "MADMAN IN A BOX".

Top left: Danny Foster in *Party Animals* (2007), Smith's first series lead.

Top right: At the docks of Calisto B, the Doctor anticipates a meeting with Gideon Vandaleur in *The Wedding of River Song* (2011).

Above: The Doctor meets young Amelia (Caitlin Blackwood) at the National Museum in *The Big Bang* (2010).

Right: The budding director checks camera angles while recording *Hide* in 2012.

Playing an extremely camp Bassoon in David Rudkin's dramatisation of *The Master and Margarita* for the NYT at the Lyric Hammersmith, Smith was singled out by *The Stage* for his "mercurial versatility and commanding stage presence." He was also spotted by former *Doctor Who* companion Wendy Padbury, then in her second career as a theatrical agent, who offered to represent him. She immediately secured Smith his first professional role as a 16-year-old gay hustler in Elyzabeth Gregory Wilder's *Fresh Kills* at the Royal Court Theatre.

Joining the National Theatre, he originated the role of Paul Danzinger in Simon Stephens' *On the Shore of the Wide World*, first at the Royal Exchange Theatre in Manchester and then at the Cottesloe Theatre on the South Bank. Within months of graduating from university, he was cast as James Lockwood in the National's 2005 UK tour of *The History Boys*, alongside Marc Elliot and Tobias Menzies. He then joined the repertory cast of *Burn/Chatroom/Citizenship*, a trio of plays for young people staged by the National Theatre at the Cottesloe.

Over the summer of 2006, Smith recorded his screen début, co-starring with Billie Piper in *The Ruby in the Smoke* and *The Shadow in the North*, television adaptations of the books by Philip Pulman. Piper played Victorian investigator Sally Lockhart in her first project since leaving the role of Rose Tyler in *Doctor Who*, while Smith played her sidekick, courageous Cockney Jim Taylor. They worked together again the following year in the sixth episode of the ITV2 series *Secret Diary of a Call Girl*.

Smith's breakout role came as one of the four leads in the BBC Two serial *Party Animals*, playing lovesick Danny Foster, a studious researcher for Labour Home Office junior minister Jo Porter (Raquel Cassidy). Early in 2007, he shot scenes for what would have been his first feature film appearance, playing Ralph Fiennes' character as a young man in Martin McDonagh's *In Bruges* (2008), but the brutal sequence was cut from the final release print.

As consolation he received rave reviews for his role as a posh cross-dressing teenager with an unhealthy addiction to his alcoholic mother (Lindsay Duncan) in Polly Stenham's play *That Face*, and then co-starred with Christian Slater in *Swimming with Sharks* at the Vaudeville Theatre in the West End. Portraying a naïve film-school graduate, Smith was seen alongside his future *Doctor Who* companion Arthur Darvill.

Late in 2008, he was the first actor to audition for the role of Dr John Watson in Steven Moffat's *Sherlock* series. Moffat felt that Smith wasn't right for Watson but casting director Andy Pryor, who'd just cast him in the BBC detective series *Moses Jones*, called him back to audition for *Doctor Who*.

"The Doctor is a very special part, and it takes a very special actor to play him," said Moffat. "You need to be old and young at the same time, a boffin and an action hero, a cheeky schoolboy and the wise old man of the universe.

OTHER ROLES

PARTY ANIMALS (2007)
In his series début, Smith played parliamentary researcher Danny, sharing a flat with his lobbyist brother Scott (Andrew Buchan) and smitten with his colleague Kirsty (Andrea Riseborough).

THE STREET: TAXI (2007)
The tenth episode of Jimmy McGovern's powerful Manchester-set series involved Smith's character being wrongly accused of battering a taxi driver to death. He also appeared briefly in the previous episode, *Demolition*.

MOSES JONES (2009)
Smith co-starred as Dan Twentyman, an ambitious young detective assigned to DI Moses Jones (Shaun Parkes) in an investigation into ritualistic killings in London's Ugandan exile community.

CLONE (aka WOMB, 2010)
In his first feature appearance, Smith played both a cockroach-breeding activist and a clone of himself who is unaware of his origins. This strange, haunting SF drama may be too languid for some but Smith's performance is stunning.

CHRISTOPHER AND HIS KIND (2011)
For his starring role as writer Christopher Isherwood, discovering gay life in 1931 Berlin, the BBC insisted that Smith shouldn't appear totally nude. "They told me I must not show Doctor Who's bare bottom," said director Geoffrey Sax.

BERT & DICKIE (2012)
The inspirational true story of Bert Bushnell (Smith) and Dickie Burnell (Sam Hoare), two young rowers thrown together as double sculls partners just five weeks before the final of the 1948 London Olympics.

As soon as Matt walked through the door, and blew us away with a bold and brand new take on the Time Lord, we knew we had our man."

After learning that Smith was to be the Eleventh Doctor, viewers were kept waiting nearly a year to see his brief initial appearance in the closing moments of *The End of Time* Part Two. His first full episode, *The Eleventh Hour*, was the 65-minute opener to the 2010 series and was watched by an audience of over ten million in the UK.

Viewers quickly warmed to Smith's eccentric portrayal of a self-styled "madman in a box" given to flashes of sartorial silliness. His floppy-haired, puppy-eyed, bandy-legged, finger-waggling hyperactivity combined the excitability of a five-year-old eating a bucket of Smarties with the social awkwardness of a closeted teenager at a Freshers' Ball.

"As the Doctor ages he gets younger and sillier," Smith told *The Guardian*. "He's over 1,000 now, I think, and I just like him, his lack of cynicism. He's like a baby. He wants to sniff, to taste, everything; he'll never dismiss anything. If the Doctor had a bath, it would be filled with rubber ducks which could talk; he'd find a way to reinvent the common bath. I admire that."

With three full series and three Christmas Specials under his belt, Smith unexpectedly announced in June 2013 that he'd decided to step down after the series' 50th anniversary episode, *The Day of the Doctor*, and one last Christmas Special. Eager to flex other creative muscles, he'd recently directed his first television film, *Cargese*, an urban drama for Sky Arts, and had just finished filming a feature role in Ryan Gosling's *How to Catch a Monster* (2014).

He shot his final scenes for *Doctor Who* on 5 October and went directly into rehearsals for *American Psycho*, playing narcissistic serial killer Patrick Bateman in a musical adaptation of the Bret Easton Ellis novel at London's Almeida Theatre.

Summing up his four years as the Doctor, Smith said, "*Doctor Who* has been the most brilliant experience for me as an actor and a bloke. It's been an honour to play this part, to follow the legacy of brilliant actors, and helm the TARDIS for a spell. But when ya gotta go, ya gotta go, and Trenzalore calls." ✻

Top: Relaxing on set with Karen Gillan and Arthur Darvill during recording of *The Power of Three* in 2012.

Above: Getting buffed up during filming of the movie *How to Catch a Monster* in 2013.

Right: Smith as Bertram Bushnell with Sam Hoare as Richard Burnell in *Bert & Dickie* (2012).

SCRIPTING THE ELEVENTH DOCTOR

The youngest-looking Doctor to date is socially awkward, but a master manipulator.

FEATURE BY **JUSTIN RICHARDS**

For all his undoubted experience and wisdom, the Eleventh Doctor often seems the most naïve and gauche incarnation of all.

The fact that he doesn't seem to 'get' human beings and modern life not only gives rise to humour, it also provides the backdrop and defining situation for *The Lodger* (2010), *Closing Time* (2011) and much of *The Power of Three* (2012). These stories are fairly straightforward adventures, the complexity arising from the Doctor's inability to 'relate', which in turn pokes fun at some of the ridiculous things we humans take for granted. This continues into the TARDIS itself via the Doctor's otherworldly response to the developing relationship between Amy and Rory.

More complex is the Doctor's relationship with River Song. Told out of sequence, the relationship is inextricably bound up in the narrative

HE'S AN ADVOCATE OF PEACE AND JUSTICE, BUT HIS ENEMIES SEE HIM AS A FORMIDABLE WARRIOR.

structure of the Eleventh Doctor's adventures. Sets of stories form narrative arcs that are far more closely bound than in previous years. The River Song story is just one thread that develops through these arcs, with each season offering a more definite and plot-based progression.

So River Song's story is firmly linked to the Doctor's own. But Amy too becomes vital to the ongoing story – and to River's own background. And the reason the Doctor befriends Clara is because he already knows from previous encounters with 'aspects' of her that she is a mystery he must solve.

As well as being intricately linked, the stories tend to be more complex in themselves. Following the success of the Tenth Doctor's *Blink* (2007), many Eleventh Doctor stories play with the narrative possibilities of time travel. Whereas before this was a rare occurrence saved for stories like *Day of the Daleks* (1972), *City of Death* (1979) or *Turn Left* (2008), it now becomes almost expected; the Eleventh Doctor isn't averse to going into his own time stream to manipulate events. For Rory in particular, this means that death isn't always forever. Clara's interventions at the end of *The Name of the Doctor* (2013) are perhaps the natural culmination of this, with versions of herself struggling to save the Doctor from danger.

Whereas the Tenth Doctor tended to get involved once a threat was already established, the Eleventh is far more caught up in events. Often, he becomes the narrative centre. Events are caused by and revolve around the Doctor himself, as in *Victory of the Daleks* (2010), *Amy's Choice* (2010), *The Pandorica Opens* (2010), *The Impossible Astronaut* (2011), *The Doctor's Wife* (2011), *A Good Man Goes to War* (2011), *Let's Kill Hitler* (2011), *The Wedding of River Song* (2011), *Asylum of the Daleks* (2012), and the whole of the Great Intelligence/Clara arc of 2013. The traveller who used to get entangled in ongoing stories has now become the story himself.

This points up a central contradiction of the Doctor's lives. He's an advocate of peace and justice, but his enemies see him as a formidable warrior. Certainly, the Great Intelligence sees itself as a victim of the Doctor's actions... And in *Dinosaurs on a Spaceship* (2012), is Solomon the villain or the victim as the Doctor engineers his destruction?

There's no doubt that Solomon starts out as the villain, yet many stories don't actually have a tangible villain as such. Even when there is a defined threat, there's often an ambiguity to the character, a question mark over whether they're broadly 'good' or 'bad'. This can be a benefit when it works well, leading to the palpable

dramatic tension of *A Town Called Mercy* (2012). But there's also a danger that the threat becomes diluted and unfocused. Whereas one of the great benefits of the preceding era was that it was obvious what had to happen for the story to end, in the Eleventh Doctor's stories it isn't always clear what the end point must be.

More than ever though, there's a sense of continuity, of progression outside the individual stories themselves. For the Eleventh Doctor more than any other, his adventures form one long, interconnected and never-ending narrative where elements bleed through from one story into future or even past adventures. ✳

"I DESTROYED ALL OF MY GEEK STUFF BECAUSE I DIDN'T WANT TO BE A GEEK."

PETER CAPALDI

The actor cast as the next Doctor already has a long and intriguing history with the show that he loves.

FEATURE BY **JONATHAN RIGBY**

It must be rare – quite probably unique – for an actor to win the title role in a television programme over 40 years after first being mentioned in production office memos.

Of course, four decades ago Peter Capaldi was a teenager and in no way a potential Doctor. But in the summer of 1972 his name did crop up from time to time, with reference to the *Doctor Who* Fan Club, in the correspondence of Sarah Newman, secretary of the show's then-producer Barry Letts.

The paper trail also includes a letter the young Capaldi wrote to the *Radio Times* in February 1974 ("May I congratulate you on your excellent *Dr Who* special... [which] has certainly made the year for *Dr Who* fans"), together with a May 1976 fanzine interview he conducted with BBC graphic designer Bernard Lodge. "Watching the abstracted light forms and patterns which appear in the opening sequence of *Dr Who*," Capaldi enthused, "has become a familiar ritual for all of us."

So, for Capaldi, there was no doubt a 40-years-on piquancy to the announcement, on 4 August 2013, that he was to become the Twelfth Doctor. The news broke amid the razzmatazz of the BBC special *Doctor Who Live: The Next Doctor*. The significance of Capaldi's triumphal entrance – clutching his lapels in the trademark style of William Hartnell – was probably lost on all but the most dedicated of *Who* connoisseurs.

The Hartnell reference was apt, given that at the time Capaldi was the same age (55) as Hartnell was when *Doctor Who* began. Of Irish-Italian extraction, Capaldi was born in Glasgow on 14 April 1958 and attended the Glasgow School of Art, moonlighting as lead singer of the punk band Dreamboys while doing so. This came at the tail end of an awkward 1970s adolescence, during which, he maintains, "Geeks hadn't been invented, so being tall and skinny, into horror movies and sci-fi and unable to play football simply made me the go-to guy for the sociopaths (some of them teachers) who wanted to practise their torturing skills on someone."

In the early 1980s, Capaldi's entry into acting was a fortuitous one. His landlady happened to be a costume designer, and when film director Bill Forsyth dropped in one day he decided the youthful Capaldi was ideal for his next project, *Local Hero*. This involved the untried actor sharing scenes with Hollywood legend Burt Lancaster.

Working to consolidate this flying start, Capaldi experienced at least as many lows as highs, the two of them colliding for his 1993 short film *Franz Kafka's It's a Wonderful Life*. As writer-director, Capaldi won a BAFTA and an Oscar, but he was unable to capitalise on its success. "I got to Hollywood and I didn't know what to do once I got there," he lamented.

Even so, Capaldi remained a presence behind the camera as well as in front of it – writing and starring in the 1992 film *Soft Top, Hard Shoulder* and serving as writer-director on the ill-fated 2001 feature *Strictly Sinatra*. The failure of the latter resulted in a particularly bleak period. "Being Scottish," he recalled, "I wore black and went into mourning for five years."

The clouds lifted in 2005 when he was cast in *The Thick of It*, Armando Iannucci's acid political satire which ran to four series and a spin-off feature film.

In retrospect, Capaldi's role as rapacious, manipulative and pathologically foul-mouthed spin doctor Malcolm Tucker seems like ideal casting. But at the time it came out of left field.

"I'm usually required to be boyish, easygoing and charming," Capaldi claimed in 2006. "So I leapt at this role. ▶

Above: Peter Capaldi as troubled Permanent Secretary John Frobisher in *Torchwood: Children of Earth* (2009).

Opposite page: Rankin's portrait of Capaldi, issued by the BBC following his announcement as the Twelfth Doctor.

Inset: Capaldi adopts a pose familiar to connoisseurs in *Doctor Who Live: The Next Doctor* (2013).

Below: Capaldi as ruthless spin doctor Malcolm Tucker in the satirical comedy *The Thick of It* (2005-12).

PETER CAPALDI

OTHER ROLES

LOCAL HERO (1983)

In his first feature, Capaldi acquitted himself well opposite veterans Burt Lancaster and Fulton Mackay. "The ones who love that film," he points out, "seem to watch it five times a year or more."

DANGEROUS LIAISONS (1988)

At the end of 1988, Capaldi was back in cinemas as the kilted hero of Ken Russell's ridiculous shocker *The Lair of the White Worm* and as John Malkovich's crafty valet, Azolan, in this lush adaptation of the Choderlos de Laclos novel.

SOFT TOP, HARD SHOULDER (1992)

Stefan Schwartz's film won Capaldi a Scottish BAFTA as Best Actor. He also wrote the partly autobiographical script, casting himself as the reluctant heir to a Glasgow ice-cream business.

THE CROW ROAD (1996)

Capaldi was cast as the errant Uncle Rory in BBC Scotland's excellent four-part adaptation of the Iain Banks novel. He was also responsible for several audiobook versions of Banks' works.

THE THICK OF IT (2005-12)

For Capaldi, the role of bile-spouting sociopathic spin doctor Malcolm Tucker was an awards-laden triumph, with the cult BBC series spinning off into a successful feature film, *In the Loop*, produced in 2008.

THE CRICKLEWOOD GREATS (2012)

As writer-director-presenter of this spoof BBC Four documentary, Capaldi attempted to encompass the entire history of the British film industry by analysing just one (completely bogus) studio.

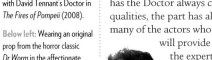

Above: Tucker intimidates Ollie Reeder (Chris Addison) in the *Thick of It* film spin-off *In the Loop* (2009).

Below: Capaldi (as Caecilius) with David Tennant's Doctor in *The Fires of Pompeii* (2008).

Below left: Wearing an original prop from the horror classic *Dr Worm* in the affectionate spoof *The Cricklewood Greats* (2012).

A year ago nobody was interested in me. I am suddenly wanted as a very bad man, rather than whatever I was before."

The combination of Capaldi's former reputation as a whimsical young lead with his latterday notoriety as the monstrous Tucker bodes well for the Twelfth Doctor. Not only has the Doctor always called for a careful mix of antithetical qualities, the part has also had a career-redefining impact on many of the actors who've played him. Maybe in this Capaldi will provide another echo of William Hartnell, the expert comic actor who passed through a middle period as a fearsome disciplinarian type before becoming the nation's favourite as the First Doctor.

On the announcement of who was to play the character's latest incarnation, it was suggested that Capaldi may retain his Scottish accent. It was also rumoured that the production team has devised a means of explaining Capaldi's appearance as a different character, Caecilius, in the 2008 story *The Fires of Pompeii*. Whatever happens, Capaldi is clearly, as Matt Smith called him, "a really canny choice."

Two days after the BBC announcement, Capaldi appeared in the pages of *The Big Issue*, reflecting ruefully on his own former incarnation as a geek. "I destroyed all my geek stuff because I didn't want to be a geek," he wrote, "and I regret it to this day." Into the flames went personal mementos of, among others, Peter Cushing, Spike Milligan, Frankie Howerd and the early Doctors. "I wish I'd known," Capaldi mused, "that one day the geek would inherit the Earth."

Just the Earth? In the case of this particular geek, make that time and space as well. ✳